from
Horseshoe to
Harpur Hill

by **Gary Gibson**

British Mountaineering Council

177–179 Burton Road, Manchester M20 2BB

Important Note

Climbing in quarries is dangerous.

None of the sites described in this book is suitable for inexperienced climbers.

Rock stability

Where sites have been worked in the past few decades, faces remain inherently unstable and subject to sudden collapse. Popularity of a route is no guarantee of its safety. Always approach quarry climbs with the same degree of anticipation as you would do any climb.

Wearing a helmet is a very good idea.

Fixed gear stability

Sport climbs feature a variety of fixed gear and lower-off points. Whilst climbers may generally assume these to be bomb-proof, there can be no guarantee that all are.

Fixed gear has been placed by a variety of individuals and methods over a long period, and it is placed to no set standard.

If an anchor is solid, do not assume that the rock it is in is also solid until you have made your own judgement.

Every climber must make a unique judgement on every ascent.

Enjoy climbing safely.

BMC Participation Statement

The BMC recognises that climbing, hillwalking and mountaineering are activities with a danger of personal injury or death. Participants in these activities should be aware of, and accept, these risks, and be responsible for their own actions and involvement.

British Mountaineering Council

PEAK SPORT CLIMBS

from
Horseshoe to
Harpur Hill

Mid-grade sport climbing
in the Buxton and
Matlock area

Volume Editor: Gary Gibson
Series Editor: Niall Grimes

Peak Sport Climbs –
From Horseshoe to Harpur Hill
Mid-grade sport climbs in the
Buxton and Matlock area

Copyright © 2004 British Mountaineering Council

Published by:
British Mountaineering Council,
177–179 Burton Road,
Manchester M20 2BB.

All rights reserved. No part of this work covered by the copyright
herein may be reproduced or used in any form or by any means –
graphic, electronic, or mechanised, including photocopying, recording,
taping, or information storage and retrieval systems – without the
written permission of the publisher.

First printed 2004

ISBN 0-903908-72-7

Cover photo: John Stanger on Full Frontal, F6c
Harpur Hill. Photo: Niall Grimes.

Produced and typeset by the British Mountaineering Council

based on original designs by
Vertebrate Graphics, Sheffield,
www.v-graphics.co.uk

Vertebrate
Graphics

Printed in Slovenia by Compass Press

Table of Contents

Introduction

Sport climbing. Bolts. Redpointing. The very words have caused a shudder and all manner of reaction through the climbing world for a number of years. There have been well-constructed and reasonable arguments for and against the possible spread of the 'problem' into areas of the Peak District deemed inappropriate for such behaviour. In some instances this escalated to a full-scale tirade of abuse and scurrilous removal, and placement, of *in-situ* protection against the wishes of all parties concerned.

Past hostilities have quietened to the point where an agreed policy and protocols for all parties has been accepted, allowing such activities to take place alongside the more traditional aspect of climbing most commonly associated with the Peak District and so fundamental to the origins of British climbing.

Many, but not all, would now agree that sport climbing in the Peak District has found an acceptable and relatively comfortable niche among the full range of British climbing styles. This does not directly conflict with its gritstone counterpart or the majority of prime traditional limestone climbing venues in the Peak: Stoney Middleton, High Tor, Beeston Tor, Staden Quarry and Chee Tor to name a few.

Whilst recognising that many parties do hold conflicting views, it was felt that the time was right to produce a guide that reflected the state of play of sport climbing on a number of limestone crags in the Peak District.

Many of these cliffs bear a strong resemblance in that the majority are worked-out quarries, now fallen into disuse and of little value to their previous owners and creators. This is not to say that all of the cliffs bear an exact likeness, nor atmosphere, nor size. There is a vast array of difference. The most popular crag of its type in the Peak District, Horseshoe Quarry, lies in complete contrast to the setting of Harpur Hill or that of Cawdor or Intake Quarry. The quarrymen have left us a wealth of choice and with it a wealth of diversity.

The climbing too has a lot to offer. Whilst there is a broad range of grades the most enticing thing is the amount of routes towards the lower end of the sport climbing grade spectrum: most climbs in this guide lie in the F6 range.

Similarly the rock varies massively in type. Some of the quarrymen have hit striking natural fault lines upon which lie glinting crystals of quartz and an abundance of unusually sculptured rock formations. Others have hit rock akin to 'ready-mix' and climbers have sought to find a way up the cliff by cleaning methods similar to the blasting that went before them.

And it has to be said, quarries in themselves can be bleak places to climb, places that a selection of the climbing public completely abhors. But these places have their uses. And the great thing is not all quarries seem just that. Some have atmosphere and character. Just choose the right crag and on a summer evening you can see the sun set behind the hillside at 10pm at night as you embark on your final route for the evening. Go out there and enjoy.

Gary Gibson

Opposite: Gary Gibson cocking a leg at the establishment on When Reason Sleeps, F7a+, Smalldale (page 113). Photo: David Simmonite.

This **book**

This book is designed, first and foremost, as a guide to sport climbing. Many of the crags covered will have traditionally-protected climbs between or in the vicinity of the bolt-protected climbs that are covered. In most cases, these traditional climbs will not be covered. It is hoped that this will not be seen as a comment on the quality, significance or value of these climbs, as they are without doubt, on a par with those climbs covered in every way. However, this guide is here to serve the growing number of climbers enjoying the new range of bolt-protected climbs now on offer in the area. To this end, only the most striking traditional climbs have been marked in the text, as a gentle reminder of what exists, and as a help to finding your way.

The coverage, based geographically on a triangle whose corners are Matlock, Buxton and Horseshoe Quarry, is biased towards those cliffs which hold climbs to interest the mid-grade sport climber; hence 'harder' crags, such as Raven Tor, and the steeper crags in Chee Dale and Water-cum-Jolly, are not covered. As well as the fact that these crags attract a very different type of climber, they are also well- covered in other recent BMC guides.

How it works
The guide makes extensive use of colour topos to supplement written text. These are designed to work together. Lines on the diagrams will give a good general idea of where a climb goes. Where needed, text will help with the finer detail. In most cases, the line will be found by following the line of bolts. Whilst every effort has been made to get all details correct, never rely solely on the line, nor try to follow it at all costs. They are there as guides, and, as with all climbing, judgment must always be used.

Important note
The inclusion of a crag or a route in this guide does not imply a right to climb. Descriptions are recorded for historical purposes only. Great effort has gone into this guide to ensure that grades and descriptions are correct, but as always, climbers must use judge-

ment to ensure that difficulties are within their capabilities, and accept the consequences of their decisions.

Neither the BMC nor anyone involved in the production or distribution of this book, accept any responsibility for any errors it may contain, nor is liable for any injuries or damages arising from its use. Climbing is a dangerous pastime.

Mark Chamberlain on Say it with Flowers, F6c, Horseshoe Quarry (page 36).
Photo: Niall Grimes.

Acknowledgements

A debt of gratitude is due to the many people who made this guidebook possible. The most humble apologies to anyone who belongs here but does not appear.

Thanks are due to
Bill Birch, Pete Cresswell, Rick Gibbon, Mike Hunt, Nadim Siddiqqui and Nick Taylor for their significant input to this book.

Illustrations
Phil Gibson has once again graced the pages of this volume with his superb crag drawings. Further photos are supplied by Tim Cresswell, Dave Parry, Carl Ryan, David Simmonite and Nick Taylor. All other artwork and uncredited photographs by Niall Grimes.

Script checking and proof reading
Helen Bush, Dave Gregory, Rick Gibbon, Peter Harrison, Guy Keating, Tony Ryan and Ian Smith.

Our thanks
to Henry Folkard and Guy Keating for their crucial input on access for this book, Frank Connel, Colin Foord and Ken Wilson for making their own particular contribution to the production of this guide, to Alex Messenger and Allen Williams for their help in the computer department, to Dominic Oughton, just for looking good, and Mary Ryan, for knowing which way is up.

BMC Guidebook Committee
John Horscroft, Mike Hunt, Dave Musgrove, Dave Turnbull and Richard Wheeldon.

A special thanks
goes out to Hazel Gibson, Helen Bush, Sophie J Cat and Lulu Dog for sharing in all the special joy that is guidebook production.

The volunteers
This guide has been produced through the voluntary effort of countless selfless individuals who freely give their time, skills, knowledge and efforts so that users can enjoy the best and most accurate guides possible. This carries on the fine tradition of volunteer-based guides which, over the years, has ensured the recording and presentation of information that is so valuable to the climbing public. Long may it remain so.

Big smiles all round

Lucian Cottle making the bold and tenuous finishing moves of Private Prosecution, F6c (page 36). Photo: Niall Grimes.

Climbing notes

Sport climbing

Sport climbing is a type of climbing that relies predominantly on the use of fixed equipment in the form of bolts and pegs for protection. This may seem to some, therefore, to be climbing without risk, but this is not the case.

As with all climbing, judgement must be employed at all times, and all effort must be made to ensure safety (see notes elsewhere).

In the text, sport climbs can be identified by the 'F' in the grade, and having their identification number inside a green circle.

Most sport routes in this guide are bolted in what most people would consider to be a normal way, with bolt spacing in line with that elsewhere. Where bolts are more spaced than normal, this will generally be mentioned in the text. If there are routes that would benefit from having supplementary natural protection, this will generally be mentioned also.

Unless mentioned, therefore, all sport routes in this guide can be led with a rack of quickdraws. Ten is

usually sufficient for most routes. A single 10 or 11mm rope is the most common choice on the crags. A 60m rope will usually permit leaders to reach the ground when lowering off, although always check the route length.

Grades

For all sport climbs in this guide, the French grading system has been used. See the grade comparison table inside the back cover for an idea of how this relates to traditional grades.

Where non-sport routes are mentioned in the text, the traditional UK system has been used. This grade will identify traditionally-protected routes as such, as will the blue identification circle used for numbers in the text and on topos.

Quality

The normal star system is used in this guide to indicate quality. All effort has been made to make sure that stars are not given away too easily. It is worth remembering that this is Peak Limestone. **This is not the south of France.**

New routes, first ascents etc.

Traditionally new routes were recorded in scruffy books in greasy cafes. Nowadays, the internet has become the medium of choice for first ascensionists. The author has maintained a website which has contained the information in this guide, and would be a good place to record new climbs (www.sportsclimbs.co.uk). Or send them to guides@thebmc.co.uk. There is also a Peak new routes register at www.ukclimbing.com.

Traditional climbs

Many of the crags covered in this guide also have long histories of traditional climbing. Only the most obvious have been covered in this volume. It is hoped that by the time this guide goes to print, there will be a web-based resource which will detail all the traditional climbing which occurs on the crags that are covered here (see www.thebmc.co.uk).

Dominic Oughton enjoying the sunshine on Downtown, F6b, on the Sanctuary area of Harpur Hill (page 136). Photo: Niall Grimes.

Traditional climbing & sport climbing

A bolter's viewpoint
by Gary Gibson

From its inception as a sport in the late 19th century, climbing has always been valued as a dangerous activity dependant on self-preservation through traditional means, those of placing your own protection whilst leading a climb. Admittedly, protection devices have advanced and improved over the years to make the sport 'safer' but this has supported the importance of this style of climbing, for which Britain is admired and revered throughout the world.

In the early 1980s, this tradition began to be threatened by a new style of climbing involving bolt protection in larger numbers than had gone before. This style of climbing was a whole new breed, termed 'sport climbing', hitherto developed on the limestone cliffs of southern France. At first these sport climbs were few and far between and always at the cutting edge of their grade and brought huge condemnation from the climbing press and public alike, all re-emphasising the traditional roots of the sport.

That which is once the preserve of the elite will soon percolate down through the system. 'Demand' increases. Sport climbs became more accepted; climbers of all abilities travel to Europe and enjoy bolt clipping vacations; with the increasing development of indoor climbing centres, the apparent demand for routes within the ability of the masses increased. What was to develop was a watershed in British climbing. Demand will lead to supply and eventually there were a handful of climbers who were prepared to develop what they though were suitable venues for this activity.

The decisions to do this were never taken lightly. All the climbers involved had long histories of traditional British climbing behind them, and were well aware of the effect that their actions might have on this tradition. However, climbing is a constantly evolving sport, so with one eye on the valued traditions, and another on the future, some climbers decided to create bolt protected routes.

One such crag was Harpur Hill, a crag previously felt to be the preserve of the traditional climber: many routes had gone before via the numerous crack-lines that festooned the quarry walls. A large number of sport routes were added which immediately incurred the wrath of the traditional climbers. These climbers were concerned that the spread of bolts could undermine the values of the sport as they saw it, and also that it negated the achievements of climbers who had gone before. The bolters, while accepting these points, had firm ideas themselves of where was legitimate to bolt and where was not. However, open warfare ensued and the bolts were unceremoniously removed by the anti-bolt fraternity, with both parties' actions leaving very bitter feelings with the other.

Luckily today common sense has prevailed and what has resulted from this 'stand-off' has been a sensible approach from both parties. A bolting policy, agreed by both sides, is now in place with acceptable venues for both traditional and sport climbing alike. Of course the unease with how further sport climbing may yet spread remains in the back of some people's minds but this cannot alter the fact that traditional climbing styles and values should remain respected in order that both types of climbing can be enjoyed without the other being compromised.

To aid this process the British Mountaineering Council have developed, through the appropriate consultation of all parties from both a traditional and sporting background, a bolting policy with clear guidance on where bolts can and can't be placed. For anybody wishing to add to the wealth of sport climbs in the Peak this should be 'the gospel' before embarking on your route to fame as should a sense of consideration for others.

The view from the other side of the fence, by Colin Foord

Colin Foord, who was involved in stripping the bolts from Harpur Hill, shares his view of the Great Harpur Hill Bolt Debate.

In the mid 1990s sport climbing activists saw this less-frequented quarry as a venue ripe for development. Harpur, however, was not a "new" crag, for since the 1960s rock climbs had been recorded here by local adventurers and the travelling curious. The quarry and its routes therefore had a recognised place in Peak District guidebooks, but undeterred by this, energetic work took place and scores of bolts with a full array of chain lower-offs adorned or violated the rock depending on individual points of view.

This action was certain to be controversial, as unlike many smooth, overhanging limestone walls where bolts had achieved a general degree of acceptance at the sharp end of technical climbing achievement, the rock here was more amenable and well endowed with cracks to take conventional protection. Harpur Hill Quarry therefore was a "normal" crag being openly subjected to "conversion", and its newly imposed ethical code was at the very least worthy of critical scrutiny.

Intensifying the challenging nature of the bolting was the way that many of the equipped routes were concentrated on formerly climbed buttresses, and to add salt to the wounds of the aggrieved, topo guides bore no indication or acknowledgement of the pre-existing climbs over and around which the new lines roamed. The sport enthusiasts saw their work as a missionary idea to provide protected climbing across the full range of grades, but others saw opportunities for future climbers being stolen in inconsiderate haste as the rock, its history, potential and the accepted ethics of rock climbing were over-written by a variant code. The irresistible drilling inevitably met an immovable outrage and battle was joined in a "bolt war" played out with religious zeal.

Direct action saw the stripping of nearly all bolts from the cliff and counter actions saw some routes stripped and re-bolted twice. Additionally, much climbing activity took place, resulting not only in new climbs but also ascents of the great majority of the formerly bolted routes using conventional gear at standards not at all excessive for the time. The subsequent re-bolting of many of these latter routes, particularly on Papacy Buttress was, and still is, as controversial as anything that happened during the whole saga. There were meetings, debates and attempts at agreements but opinions were entrenched. Beliefs relating to the place of sport climbing within British Mountaineering were presented and tested in cauldrons of argument. The chief protagonists on both sides had steadfast conviction and remain unrepentant. It will be interesting to see how future generations judge their respective actions.

After a year or two of virtual stalemate and comparative inactivity the sport climbing potential of Harpur Hill was looked at again and further equipping has taken place with an apparent degree of sympathy for traditional rock climbing as prominent crack-lines have been left largely untouched. Those who have elected to create the bolt protected routes have accepted a heavy responsibility in respect of their judgement of the need for their creations. If subsequent usage is low, their work might be seen as squandering tomorrow's adventure resource for the purpose of today's indulgence.

Deeds however have been done, for it seems to be in the nature of Harpur Hill that people have seldom been shy about nailing colours to the mast. We currently have at our disposal a seething mixture of intermingled traditionally protected and sport climbing with good things to suit most tastes- including historians and politicians. The peace is still a little sensitive, and past furore ensures that both current and future use of the quarry will always be under a spotlight.

Ian Loombe on Running Man, F6b,
at Horseshoe Quarry (page 41).
Photo: David Simmonite.

Dave Smith cranking through the crux bulge on Full Frontal, F6c (page 129). Photo: Niall Grimes.

Access and conservation notes

The inclusion of a crag or a route in this book does not imply any right to climb there.

For most crags in this book, no formal access agreements exist. Climbing activity has been actively discouraged or apparently tolerated with different degrees from site to site.

If you are asked to leave, it would be prudent to do so without much fuss since you almost certainly have no right to be there. It would be helpful if you could inform the BMC if you experience any particular problems. (tel. 0870 010 4878; www.thebmc.co.uk)

The BMC website also has a Regional Access Database which aims to keep-up-to date access information. It may well be worth consulting before a visit. The railway line below Devonshire Buttress, Blackwell Halt and Blatant Buttress is a live line. Crossing it is both dangerous and illegal.

Environment
Convenience parking and other roadside behaviour have unnecessarily exacerbated local access difficulties in some places. Be discreet and considerate of others.

Disused quarries can rapidly develop a splendid and specialist flora, and act as a haven and magnet for all sorts of wildlife. This is every bit as valuable to ecologists (and many climbers) as the climbing is to you. Respect their values and there is a better chance others will respect yours.

Other useful information

Pubs & cafes
For the tired, the hungry and the thirsty, here are a few recommendations:

Horseshoe Quarry
Traditionally, the Moon Inn on Stoney High Street

was the boozer of choice, although the Three Stags Heads at Wardlow Mires is a far superior experience, if you get it open. Stoney also has a good fish and chip shop, and the famed Lover's Leap cafe, steeped richly in climbing mythology, is open once more. There is also a good cafe in the filling station opposite the Three Stags at Wardlow. For coffees and cakes, the Outside shop at Calver is a good option, as you can also go and spend money in the shop after.

Matlock area
The fleshpots of Matlock Bath await the unsuspectiong visitor to the area, with its greasy chips and its cheap beer. However, the more discerning visitor will enjoy the wonderful Barley Mow at Bonsal, just up the hill from Slaley, with great beer and live music at weekends. For Intake, try the Barley Mow at Kirk Ireton, a decidedly low-tec delight, with beer coming up from the cellar in jugs. The Rising Sun is also decent. For eating, take your chances on the aforementioned chippies, or try the transport cafe

mentioned in the Slaley introduction. By far the best cafe in the area, however, is in Elton, with best chips and cakes in the Peak, and a fire in winter.

Buxton area

In Buxton itself, The George Hotel, opposite the opera house, is a good venue, with good beer and

occasional events. More cultured mid-grade sport climbers may wish to go and catch an opera after a heavy session at Harpur Hill. For food, Cafe Nat's is a great venue, open to 10 most nights, serving quality food in a relaxing setting. It lies on Market Street, which is just off the market square on the corner of Jo Royle's shop. Harpur Hill has a decent transport cafe right by the parking, with usual morning and afternoon opening, and the Traveller's Rest, a few miles away on the A53 is a splended hostelry, with good beer and food. Food can also be had on mornings and afternoons from Ancie's caravan, usually parked above Chee Dale in the Upper Toley Pike parking.

Climbing supplies

Climbing supplies can be had from Jo Royle's, 6 Market Square, Buxton (01298 25824), and from Outside in Hathersage (01433 651963). Outside also have a branch at Calver.

Mountain Rescue and First Aid

Dial 999 and ask for Police – Mountain Rescue. **Briefly describe the nature of the incident and give the crag name and OS map reference as listed at the start of each crag section.**

The Police will co-ordinate the Mountain Rescue team and, if appropriate, the county air ambulance that is available for evacuations from the crag. The local team is based in Buxton. Although **they should not be contacted directly for call-outs**, they are very happy to hear from anyone wishing to support their voluntary efforts:

Buxton Mountain Rescue Team,
8a Halsteads, Dove Holes, Buxton, Derbyshire SK17 8BJ (01298 812232), www.buxtonmrt.org.uk

Likewise, anyone wishing to support the County Air Ambulance might like to contact them at:
Staffordshire County Air Ambulance,
Appeals Headquarters, Burton Road, Dudley, West Midlands DY1 3BB (01384 241133).

FIRST AID in case of ACCIDENT

1. If spinal injuries or head injuries are suspected do not move the patient without skilled help, except to maintain breathing and circulation.
2. If breathing has stopped, clear airways and commence CPR (cardio-pulmonary resuscitation). Do not stop until expert opinion diagnoses death.
3. Stop bleeding by applying direct pressure.
4. Summon help.

These are the basic principles of first aid. If you climb at all regularly, you should seriously consider taking a first aid course. Learning enough to save a life isn't at all difficult and one day you might be very glad that you (or someone else) did.

Right: Phil Gibson on Who Flung Dung, F6b+ at Intake Quarry (page 83). Photo: Niall Grimes.

Graded List

F4

A Tracky Little Problem
Citizen's Edge
Luke Skywalker
Klingon
Sago Slab
Nit-Wit
Dream Topping

F4+

Sag Ponir
Spare Rib
Expecting
Jelly Tots
Christmas Pudding
The Height Below
The Naked Spur
Slab Cake

F5

A Tracky Little Bleeder
Saturn's Ring
The Clumps
People Will Talk
Ma Pechere
Gone for a Tim Burton
Excavator
Beam me Across Scotty
The Golden Goose
First Pryse
Join the Dots
Tiny Tots
Overbored
Slam the Jam
X Marks the Spot
Trog
Unbalanced
Ichabod
The Cake Walk

Neanderthal
It's a Steal
Opening Call
Sock It To 'em
Snap Decision

F5+

Always Break the Rules
Peckling Fever
Great White
Chauvi's Slab
For the Good of the
    Cause
The Hollow Man
The Rising Sun
Top Totty
Cry on My Hard
    Shoulder
The Porn Curtain
Bearly

F6a

Pale Rider
In the Gravy
Coral Seas
Clotted Cream
Toy Story
Dapper Dan
Foreign Tongues
Apologia
The Big Fat Texan on a
    Corner
The Christian Salvage
    Man
Simply Carp
eXit Stage Left
Just Passing Through
Vogon
Different Seasons
The Big Take Out

Sleepy Hollow
A Right Earful
Breast is Best

F6a+

By Zeus
Sir Pryse
Windows 95
Chocopotamus
Poached Please
Porgi Amor
Scales of Justice
The Candy Man
George Stark Calling
Family Ties
Lady Luck
Flossy's Slab
Omega 13
Bladrunner
Bag of Bones

F6b

Wall of Jericho
Blue Sunday
Chop Suicide
Yours Truly
Feeding Frenzy
Mega Byte
Monkey Stole my
    Walkman
Therapy
Open Season
Plum Tuckered Out
The Age of Reason
Feel the Beat
Over the Deadline
Pillar of Wisdom
For Haven's Sake
Iron Curtain
Agony Ant

What Lies Beneath
Stone the Crows
Shanacie
More Chattery Teeth
Apollo Creed
Sack of Stones
Outer Limits
The Dark Half
Tokenism
A Sharp Intake of
    Breath
Calci Mauve
Feel My Presence
The Calacspa

F6b+

Rotund Rooley
Savage Girth
Eye Catching Cod Piece
The Spectre
Pier Review
Spectre vs. Rector
Mr Love Pants
Frozen Moment
Infantada
Exclusion Zone
Megalithic Man
Screaming Wheels
Arapaho Connection
Every Breath you Take
Burning Spirits
The Quartz Tricycle
Rocky Variations
Shot Yer Bolt
The Leading Line

F6c

Rainbow Warrior
Run For Your Wife
Skin Flint

Full Frontal
Would you like a Sweety
Wild Strawberries
Learn the Lingo
Orange Alert
Great Expectations
Mouse Hunt
Legal Action
Succulent Rib
Strangled at Birth
Over the Hill
Red X
Going Straight
Prawn Crackers
Stinking Rose
Private Prosecution
Hard Drive
Secret Agenda
Reservoir Frogs
Riding the Bullet
Rain Dance
Four Telling Tales
God is Good
The Calc Spur
From Cradle to Grave
A Fossil on Fossils

F6c+

Ring Thane
Megalithic Man Super-Direct
Saweno Gancho
The Crinoid Smile
Micro Chip
Demon
Shattered
Cawdor Nothing
Simonstown
All Mine
Southern Discomfort
Sliver

Run for your Wife
The Orangeman
Labour Relations
Brazilian Style
Born Slippy
An Ancient Rhythm
Tucker's Grave
Take Flight
Dead Ringer
The Crystal Maze
Cairn
Payback

F7a

The Cutting Crew
Raven Calling
Clockwork Orange
Top MarX
Demolition Man
Mr Blue Sky
The Prophecy
Last Man First
Shore Leave
Can Boys
Here
Our Kid's Orchid
Loco-Motion
Poisonality
Lies and Deception
Larium
Trotskyism
The Bear Necessities
Too Monsterosity
Hide and Peek
First Offence
Stealth
The Light
Intolerable Cruelty
Flatworld
Much Monkey Magic

F7a+

Fisherman's Friend
Mumble Jumble
Spooktakula
You Know U.F.O.s
You've Been Tangoed
Lost Contact
The Streaming Dream
Totally Wired
Malcolm X
Southern Man
Soft Centre
Unpealed
Emission Control
Otto di Catania
Stainsby Girls
The Dark Side of the Room
The Main Motor Mile
The Streaming Dream
When Reason Sleeps
That'll Teach 'em
Obelix
The Coldfish

F7b

Certificate X
Go Your Own Way
Thirsty Work
XXXX
Virtual Insanity
In The End
Getafix
Little Blue Lies
Valley of the Birds
Jewfish
Cause Célèbre
Sample the Mantel
Mesmerised
Orange Outang

F7b+

The Beast
Power of Soul
Ratline
Y Should I
Soggy Biscuits
Wet yer Whistle

F7c

Laughing at the Rain
Squealer

F7c+

Pingham's Roof

Horseshoe Quarry

Climbers enjoying evening sunshine on
the Main Wall of Horseshoe Quarry.
Photo: Niall Grimes.

Horseshoe Quarry

O.S. Ref. **SK208761**   Altitude: **250m a.s.l.**

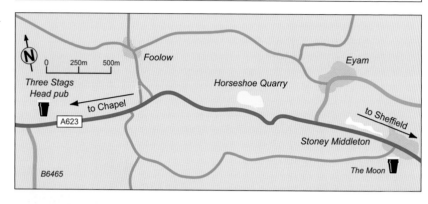

Horseshoe Quarry has the honour of being the most famous and popular quarry of its type in the Peak District. From the humble beginnings of 1985, when the quarry was first developed for its Main Wall attributes - good quality rock and long technical lines - it has now developed into a very popular venue.

Now almost worked out to its full potential, the quarry offers an array of routes so vast that it caters for almost every taste. The Main Wall routes have not changed their character but the surrounding cliffs have seen fine new routes in the lower F6 grades and the slabby back walls offer a new dimension with a collection of much easier sport routes.

The climbing

A great crag for those operating in the F6a - F6c range, with a small number of F7s, as well as about 20 F4s and F5s. The majority of the climbs are fairly technical wall climbs on good rock, with the highest concentration of good routes being on the Main Wall. Besides the vertical, there are a few overhanging climbs on Heart Buttress, as well as a number of slabbier climbs.

Note: Unfortunately the quarry has a few terrors

where first ascensionists have taken the search for new routes to a different level. Some hollow, and in places loose, rock still remains and these routes should be treated with caution and are marked as such in the text. However, as with all climbing, both climbers and belayers should be paying close attention at all times to ensure safety.

Conditions & aspect

The walls face in 3 directions, so there will always be something in the sun or the shade. The quarry takes virtually no seepage, and with its quick drying nature, is an ideal winter, spring and autumn venue, especially if the sun comes out. However, it can feel chilly when a cold winter wind is howling around the quarry. In the summer months it can be a bit too warm in the full glare of the sun on the Main Wall, although this can be avoided by going there early or by going to one of the shadier walls.

Parking & approach

The entrance to the quarry lies on the north side of the A623, 1km west of the Eyam junction (the B6521), just past a horseshoe bend, and 1km east of the Foolow turn-off. Parking exists just inside the quarry turn-off, a rough quarry track (4 cars). There is more parking on a rough lay-by 50m up the road

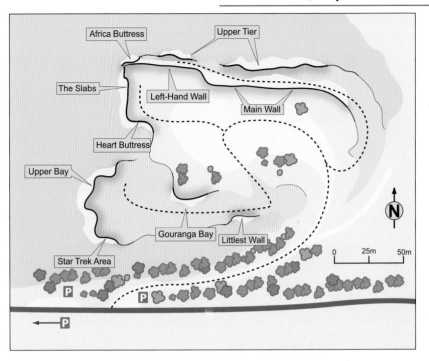

towards Foolow, and more again in a larger lay-by on the opposite side of the road. From any of these, follow the blocked-off quarry track through the trees to

the crags. **Walk-in:** all are about 5 minutes.

Traditional climbs

Horseshoe Quarry has a long tradition of naturally protected climbing. It was first developed at a time when placing a bolt only happened when there was no other form of protection (and not always then); this resulted in bold tradionally protected routes, and routes with sportingly placed bolts.

Some of the older peg and bolt protected routes have been retrobolted somewhat. Most have been left with their original character. The quarry is also host to many fully traditionally protected climbs. These take the cracks and faces between the bolt routes, and often provide good routes. Only the most significant have been included in this book. See the main introduction for further information on the traditional climbs in the areas covered in this volume.

Horseshoe Quarry Access

The position on access to Horseshoe Quarry (officially known as Furness Quarry) is evolving as this guide goes to print.

The BMC is seeking to negotiate the acquisition of most of the climbing areas. If these negotiations are successful they will own essentially the Main Wall right of Pale Rider, the tier above it, and the land you pass through between the main road and those climbing areas (both above and below the path from the road). The BMC hopes to enter into a partnership with the Derbyshire Wildlife Trust on the management of any land they acquire.

If the negotiations fail it is unlikely there will be any agreed right of access.

All the land between the right wall of Gouranga Bay and Pale Rider, including Heart Buttress, the Slabs, Africa Buttress and the Left-Hand Walls, plus the land above it, is separately owned. The owner's position here is currently that this is private land and that no access has ever been granted to it for any reason, and that no such access is likely to be granted.

In the event of acquisition, the BMC wish to point out that they do not accept any responsibility for the maintenance or integrity of fixed equipment.

**Below: Richie Sanderson on Shanks,
F6a (page 42). Photo: Niall Grimes.**

Keefe Murphy on
The Colostomy Finish, F6c+ (page 35).
Photo: Niall Grimes.

The Lower Tier

The best feature to start from is the large slabby area at the back of the quarry (the Slabs). Left of this is the Heart Buttress, and left again is a small sheltered bay.

Gouranga Bay

This slabby wall is situated directly opposite the Main Wall at the back of a recessed bay, and offers a few worthwhile morsels. The namesake route is the main prize. Good rock requiring good dry conditions. Not a winter or humid weather venue.

The wall faces east and gets early morning sun.

① Bad Boys Ink   **F6a+**
10m A barely worthwhile climb taking the shallow black groove.
Gary Gibson, 2001

② Unruly Behaviour   **F6a+**
9m A very minor route with two hard moves.
Gary Gibson, 2001

③ Treatment   **F6b**
12m Again, a route that is just about worth doing. The left-hand side of the black face to the right is taken direct at the start. That means not using the wide crack on the left!
Gary Gibson, 2001

④ Therapy   ★ **F6b**
12m The right-hand side of the smooth-looking black face. Good moves, where a long reach helps.
Simon Lee, 1993

⑤ Porgi Amor   ★ **F6a+**
12m The left-hand groove-line of two gives an interesting challenge, especially in clipping the bolts.
Nadim Siddiqui, 1998

⑥ Foreign Tongues   ★ **F6a**
12m The right-hand of the two shallow groove-ines, gained from slightly to the left. Good climbing.
Gary & Hazel Gibson, 2001

⑦ Gouranaga (Be Happy)   ★ **F6c**
12m Fine technical climbing which is unfortunately short lived. High in grade.
Nadim Siddiqui, Nick Colton, 1998

Heart Buttress

The only overhanging wall in the quarry abuts the prominent slabs at the back of the bay. Rarely dry in the winter months and after long periods of the rain.

The wall faces east and gets early morning sun.

A series of blocks below the wall form an obvious ramp with a fixed rope above it. The routes are described from the foot of this ramp.

⑧ Tors Colon   **F6c+**
12m The arête is taken on its right-hand side after 5m. Sustained, fingery and worthwhile.
Gary Gibson, Tim Parkinson, 2001

⑨ Vent Your Spleen   ★ **F7b**
12m A very bouldery start gives way to fingery and sustained upper walls.
Gary Gibson, Dave Law, 1998

The Slabs

The series of vegetated-looking slabs at the far end of the quarry and forming its back wall has yielded, somewhat surprisingly, a number of easier grade sport climbs in the F4 and F5 category. These have become quite popular due to their pleasant easier-angled nature, length and lack of such grades in the Peak District. The routes generally take the clean strips between the main vegetated patches.

WARNING: NOT ALL OF THE ROUTES ARE SOLID AND IT IS ADVISABLE FOR ALL CLIMBERS TO WEAR HELMETS ESPECIALLY WHEN BELAYING BELOW THESE ROUTES.

The wall faces east and gets early morning and afternoon sunshine, and seems to be permanently sheltered from the wind.

The first three routes are situated in the left-hand corner of the quarry. A prominent arête and two 'strips' of slab are obvious.

⑩ Heart to Heart   E4 6a
12m The straight crack to the right varies from finger-width to hand-size. This is potentially a very good traditional climb, although the crack tends to be full of dirt.
Mark Pretty, Ian French, Chris Wright, 1986

⑪ Sliver   ★ ★ F6c+
12m When dry, this fine route gives a superbly sustained jug and jam fest.
Gary Gibson, Dave Law, 1998

⑫ The Stomach Pump   F7b
11m The thin crack springing from the top of the pile of blocks. Desperate, but well-constructed!
Gary Gibson, 1998

⑬ Skin Flint   ★ F6c
11m Or flinted skin? The smooth-looking wall with a hard start and an airy, open finale.
Gary Gibson, 1998

⑭ The Blood Bank   F6b
12m This climb is gained from the top of the mud slope left of Sharing Best Practice. A hard start leads to easier climbing above.
Gary Gibson, 2001

① Sharing Best Practice   F6b
15m This prominent arête provides not so prominent climbing quality.
Gary Gibson, 2001

② Barney Rubble   F5+, F5
32m The left-hand line gives a poorer climb. The route can be climbed in one or two pitches, stopping at the half-height ledge if so desired.
Mike Hunt, Jane Livingstone, 2001

③ Chauvi's Slab   F5, F5+
32m Another route that can be split into two pitches, taking the right-hand and better of two cleaned pillars. Feels a little bold due to the spacing of the bolt runners, despite the fact that there are 13 of them!
Mike Hunt, Jane Livingstone, 2001

④ Trog   F4, F5
38m A long two-pitch route based around the slabby wall system 8m to the left of the arête. Belay in a cave behind a tree. Needs more cleaning / traffic and hence an alert belayer.
Mike Hunt, Jane Livingstone, 2001

5 Neanderthal F4, F5

38m A similar route to Trog, but slightly better, this time based around the prominent arête to the right of that climb. The same rules apply to the alertness of the belayer.

Mike Hunt, Jane Livingstone, 2000

To the right of the main slab is a subsidiary set of slabs, funnelling upwards towards the mythical Chocolate Blancmange Gully. These routes are by far the cleanest of the climbs on the slabs, and are getting better. This does not preclude the same warnings as before.

6 Excavator ★ F5

32m This is the long slim slab to the right, beginning at the foot of the slope. The best route on the slabs but you need a 70m rope to get back down the pitch in one.

Gary Gibson / Mike Hunt, Jane Livingstone, 1998

7 Slab Cake F4+

28m The direct line up the strip of slab to the right provides another pleasant outing. A 60m rope just suffices for lowering-off.

Mike Hunt, Jane Livingstone, 1999

8 Spare Rib F4+

28m This route takes the right-hand branch off the main line of Slab Cake, to climb a protruding rib.

Mike Hunt, Jane Livingstone, 1999

9 The Cake Walk F5

22m The well-cleaned central slab gives another pleasant outing.

Gary Gibson, 2001

10 Christmas Pudding F4+

18m Identifiable by a prominent ledge at 4m. The slab above needs a little / lot more cleaning.

Luke Hunt, Mike Hunt, 2001

The final two routes of the slab have a belay and retreat anchor below them.

11 Sago Slab F4

15m The left-hand of the two strips of slab.

Dave Glover, Mike Hunt, Jane Livingstone, 1999

12 Dream Topping F4

12m Pleasant and clean climbing up the right-hand strip of slab.

Mike Hunt, Jane Livingstone, Dave Glover, 1999

Africa Buttress

This buttress is situated in the top right-hand corner of the quarry and so called because it is said to be shaped like the continent in question. It also has the same colour as some of its deserts and a similar rock texture! The face consists of two walls, the lower providing a number of pleasant routes which give access to several more on the upper face. As such, combinations give good two-pitch experiences. Routes can also be reached by abseil from above.

Chocolate Blancmange Gully

50m, Scottish IV or Jackson 5.

This unique expedition takes the attractive mud-slope at the extreme left-hand end of the quarry. Climb the mud-slope until progress is halted by a suspect boulder. Climb onto this, then transfer onto the right wall of the gully. Follow a series of delectable mud bands and rock steps, trending right, until a final corner / flake can be gained to finish.

C Jackson, R Conway, R Small, November 1982

A slither into the unknown slipping boldly where no man, or indeed woman, has gone before. The first ascensionist wore wellingtons and used sharpened limestone mud tools. This is now considered 'de rigueur'.
From the 1987 Stoney Limestone guide

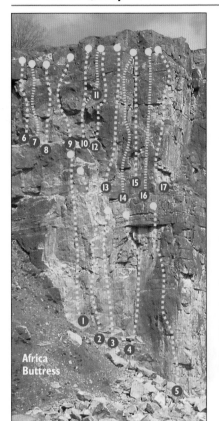

The buttress faces south and gets the sun in the afternoon and evening.

The lower face has a prominent left-hand arête.

① Out of Africa   F6b
11m Reasonably enjoyable climbing on the left-hand side of the arête.
Dave Williams, Geoff Middlehurst, Steve Beswick, 2002

② Madagascar   F6a+
11m The right-hand side of the prominent arête gives only a couple of hard moves. Disappointing.
Dave Williams, Geoff Middlehurst, 2002

③ Bird Island   F6a
12m The main corner-line. A poor route but does give easy access to the pitches above Rainbow Warrior.
Dave Williams, Geoff Middlehurst, 2002

④ Seychelles   F6b
12m A layback corner to a ledge and then a crack complete with overlap. Worthwhile, just.
Dave Williams, 2002

⑤ Rainbow Warrior   ★ F6c
15m A fine route based on the left-hand side of the lower rounded arête. Difficult at a thin crack low down with a fine finish over the 'crozzled' overlap.
Bill Birch, Rick Gibbon, 1998

The next series of routes is gained from the ledge across the top left-hand corner of the wall. This can be gained from the routes below or via an abseil from the top. The routes here are short and relatively unworthwhile.

⑥ Elizabethville   F6a
9m The left edge of the wall utilising its left-hand arête. Tricky for 2m!
Dave Williams, Geoff Middlehurst, 2002

7 Burundi   **F6b**
9m Short but packs a punch. A very thin crack 5m right of the left edge of the wall.
Dave Williams, Geoff Middlehurst, 2002

8 Townships   **F6c+**
9m A short desperate sequence on the next little wall. The 2m rule applies!
Gary Gibson, 2003

9 Victoria Falls   **F6a**
9m The layback groove to the right.
Dave Williams, Geoff Middlehurst, Mark Boulton, 2002

10 Kariba   **F6a+**
10m The steep crack has a hard move to gain a ledge.
Dave Williams, Geoff Middlehurst, 2002

11 Zanzibar   **F6b**
10m A poor eliminate requiring a direct start. Step right out of Kariba, move up, and finish almost on Simonstown.
Dave Williams, Geoff Middlehurst, 2002

12 Simonstown   ★ **F6c+**
11m The rightmost route from a slightly lower ledge. One significant hard move in a fine position.
Dave Williams, Geoff Middlehurst, 2002

The next series of routes is situated above the ledge atop Rainbow Warrior. They can be gained via that route or others below.

13 Ring Thane   ★ ★ **F6c+**
12m A super pitch, the best hereabouts. It takes the striking arête left of Pretoria and requires 5 RP5s for the ENP placements, now don't you wish you had them?
Bill Birch, Rick Gibbon, 1998

14 Pretoria   **F6b+**
12m The right-hand side of the arête forming the left wall of Mombassa. Poor.
Dave Williams, Geoff Middlehurst, 2002

15 Mombassa   **F6a**
12m The crack and corner above the lower walls.
Dave Williams, Geoff Middlehurst, 2002

16 Greenpeace   **F6a**
12m The centre of the wall right of the corner.
Bill Birch, Rick Gibbon, 1998

17 Bird Island   **F6a**
12m The right arête of the wall.
Dave Williams, 2002

Left-Hand Walls

These are the slightly recessed walls that sit to the left of the Main Wall, giving a number of easier grade sport climbs developed mainly as an add-on to the Main Wall or as a result of the foot-and-mouth disease epidemic in 2001! Here will be found a number of relatively poor routes and in some cases poor rock but mixed in amongst them are some good pitches. You can decide. On a more positive note, they do dry quickly.

The wall faces south and gets afternoon and evening sun.

The first route is situated in the back of the bay to the right of Africa Buttress.

1 Sahara   **F6c**
18m The prominent arête has some hollow holds high up and may not be suited to those of a nervous disposition. Dangerous.
Gary Gibson, 2003

2 Bloodguard   **F6c**
18m An isolated pitch 10m to the right, starting atop a mound of rubble. A short, difficult and bold sequence. The first bolt is missing at present, so be careful.
Bill Birch, Stuart Coleman, Dave Mercer, 1998

3 Grab Your Mandrakes   **F6b**
15m The right-hand side of the prominent arête and the wall above the roof. Worthwhile.
Gary & Hazel Gibson, 2002

4 Tirfin USA   **F6a**
15m The prominent angled corner-line leads to the belay of Turf's High.
Dave Williams, Geoff Middlehurst, Mark Boulton, 2001

Left-Hand Walls

5 Turf's High   **F6a+**
15m The grey, slabby wall to the right gives a couple of noteworthy moves.
Dave Williams, Geoff Middlehurst, 2001

6 Race of the Freuds   **F6b+**
18m The sinuous crack with an overlap that provides the crux moves. The slabby walls above lead to the belay.
Nick Taylor, 2000

7 Peckling Fever   ★ **F5+**
18m The short wall and crack-line lead to an overlap.
Nick Taylor, 2000

8 Senter Home   **F6a**
18m The obvious ramp / groove-line to the right leads to an overlap. A difficult finish can be taken direct or to the right.
Dave Williams, Geoff Middlehurst, 2001

9 Tirfer Off   **F6a+**
18m The shallow groove and slab immediately to the right.
Dave Williams, Geoff Middlehurst, 2001

10 Maillon Sunday   **F6b**
18m A rightwards, dogleg line with the crux after the second 'joint'. Easier above.
Dave Williams, Geoff Middlehurst, 2001

The next series of routes is situated 10m to the right and just right of a prominent corner-line. A distinguishing feature here is a prominent borehole.

11 Foul's Bane   **F6a+**
15m Just right of the slim corner-line. Finish right of the obvious roof to a belay above.
Bill Birch, Rick Gibbon, 1998

12 Drool Rock Worm   **F6b**
12m The slim wall to the left of the borehole leads to a belay below a tree.
Bill Birch, Rick Gibbon, 1998

13 Stonethroat   **F6b+**
12m The white wall to the right of the prominent borehole in the centre of the face. The best of the trio hereabouts.
Rick Gibbon, Bill Birch, 1998

14 Mr Cellulite's Arête   **F6a+**
11m It had to be said. Reach dependent. Easier if you are the BFG.
Gary & Hazel Gibson, 2001

15 Bandolier   **F6a**
15m The rightwards-facing slim corner-line to the right.
Gary & Hazel Gibson, 2001

16 The Little Thin Mexican across the Border
F6b

15m The wall to the right gains the left-hand side of a nose and an off-balance finale. A great name.
David Simmonite, Duncan Frisch, 1990

17 Desperate Measures   **F6b**

15m This route lies just left of a shattered section and has golden bolt runners. Harder climbing on the right-hand side of the sharp arête / nose. Finish as for the last route.
Gary Gibson, 2001

18 The Mexican takes Lexicon   **F6a+**

12m A pleasant steep route on solid flat holds. A good warm up.
Gary Gibson, Nick Taylor, 2003

19 Exceeding the Speed Limit   **F6b+**

15m Poorly bolted low down. Situated in the back of a slight bay to the right and with good moves high up.
David Simmonite, 1990

20 Mind Your Head   **F6b+**

12m The name applies. Straight up the wall just to the left of a slim corner. Some hollow holds.
Gary Gibson, 2003

21 Collared   **F6a**

12m The slightly steeper wall to the right with a few fragile holds low down.
Gary Gibson, 2002

22 Spare Rib   **F6b**

12m Much better. The gold-flecked wall to the right and behind an elderberry tree. A hard start leads to juggy climbing above.
Graham Wolstencroft, Mark Boulton, 2000

23 Pelvic Thrust   **F6b**

12m The scarred wall to the right and left of the slim corner. Not for the faint of heart.
Gary Gibson, Nick Taylor, 2002

24 Due Care and Attention   **F6a**

15m A short wall and groove / crack-line lead to an overlap. The steep crack above leads to the belay.
Al Churcher, 1987 / Gary Gibson, 2003

25 Any Old Iron   **F6a**

15m The short wall, flake and short arête above, all in the left wall of a slim corner. Named from an old piece of ironmongery found in the quarry and now in the route!
Gary Gibson, Tim Parkinson, Nick Taylor, 2001

㉖ Sunday Sport　　　　**F6b**

15m The slim corner is polished and leads to a high belay after a short tricky section.
Mark Pretty, 1987

㉗ Austin Powers　　　　**F6b**

18m The slim groove in the right arête of the corner, finishing via an arête on hollow holds. High in the grade and worthwhile.
Gary Gibson, Nick Taylor, 2001

㉘ The Big Fat Texan on a Corner
　　　　　　　　　　★ **F6a**

18m The centre of the clean white wall to the right. Not taken direct and with a few bold moves high up. Pleasant.
David Simmonite, Nigel Smart, 1990

Combining the start of Austin Powers along with the finish of The Big Fat Texan on a Corner gives the very cleverly titled **Austin Texas** (F6b), the best way up the wall.

㉙ He Seems So Sumo　　　　**F6a**

18m Steep and sustained climbing on the borehole / crack-line.
Gary Gibson, Nick Taylor, 2004

㉚ Olive Oil　　　　**F5+**

18m A worthwhile wall climb to the right and left of the main angle of the bay. Keep direct on the line of bolts.
Dave Williams, 2001

㉛ Removal Men　　　　**F6a**

18m Appropriately named. The large chimney in the back of the bay.
Dave Williams, 2001

㉜ Some Place　　　　**F6a+**

18m The wider crack to the right followed by an arête and crack just to the left.
Dave Williams, 2001

㉝ Sag Ponir　　　　★ **F4+**

15m The crack in the left-hand side of the arête. One hard move.
Gary Gibson, 2002

The Main Wall - Megalithic Sector

The next section of crag, the impressive expanse of flat wall, provided the main interest of development in the mid 'eighties and still provides the quarry's best routes. Most of these may be found to be a little under-bolted by some modern standards but the angle of the wall gives many an opportunity to rest and consider one's options whilst climbing. Many of the routes have a good big feel about them.

The main features of the wall are a prominent bore-hole towards its right-hand side and an impressive lead-line crack towards its left. Old 'Climbing Prohibited' graffiti still adorns the walls but these are fading fast, as are their memories. The routes begin at the arête on the left.

The walls face south, and get afternoon and evening sunshine. They take virtually no seepage.

❶ Pale Rider　　　　★ **F6a**

15m The left-hand arête of the main wall taken direct after the break. Using the crack to the right spoils the route somewhat.
Gary Gibson, 2001

❷ Rain Dance　　　　★ ★ **F6c**

18m Excellent face climbing with a hard start and rightwards finish on the headwall. This route begins 3m left of a faint left-facing corner line. There are two alternative finishes to this route, **The Colostomy Finish**, F6c+, up the arête, and **Physical Fizz,** F6c+, a highly technical wall to the right, which is hard for the grade.
Ian French, Chris Wright, 1985

❸ School's Out　　　　★ **F6b**

18m A fairly tricky start via a faint rib gains a good ledge. The scoop above leads to a pleasant finishing crack.
Ian Riddington, Geoff Radcliffe, 1985 / Gary Gibson, 2002

❹ Rotund Roolay　　　　★ **F6b+**

18m Originally a sandbag at F6b! Technical and surprisingly sustained in its upper section via a scoop and rib.
Mark Pretty, Dave Whaley, Johnny Dawes, 1986

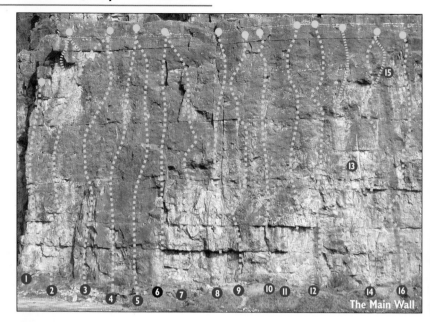

The Main Wall

5 Waves of Mutilation   **F7a**

18m The wall to the left of a thin crack provides a desperate fingery sequence. Amusing.
Simon Lee, 1993 / Gary Gibson, 2002

6 First Day of Winter   **HVS 5b**

18m The thin crack-line to the right has an awkward start and pleasant climbing above.
Bill Gregory, E Taylor, 1986

7 Wall of Jericho   ★ **F6b**

18m One of the easiest sport routes on the wall. A hard start leads to delightful climbing above. A good introduction to bolt clipping.
Steve France, Chris Wright, Ian French, 1986

8 The Leading Line   ★ **F6b+**

18m The long 'lead-line' crack gives a surprising find. Interesting manoeuvres and a long reach for the crux.
Gary Gibson, Steve Lunt, Keith Redhill, 2002

9 Say it With Flowers   ★ **F6c**

18m Again, typical of the wall. The face 5m right of the lead-line crack gives a very trying move just above

half-height.
Mark Pretty, Ian French, John Godding, 1986

10 Legal Action   ★ ★ **F6c**

18m A sustained face climb with loads of rests. Start via a short, left-facing flake and continue direct. Excellent. Your first F6c?
Chris Jackson, Bob Conway, 1984

11 Run For Your Wife   ★ ★ **F6c+**

18m Another fine, intricate test-piece, typical of the wall. The bulge above the prominent right-facing flake provides the difficulties. Keeping direct to the bolt line above provides continued entertainment.
Mark Pretty, Chris Plant, 1987

12 Private Prosecution   ★ ★ **F6c**

18m Superb varied climbing. A new start, coupled with a technical scoop and airy finish on the headwall.
Ian French, Steve France, 1986 / Gary Gibson, 1998

13 Litany Against Fear   ★ **F6c**

18m Starts by an elderberry bush. Straightforward climbing leads to a hard bulge and a new direct

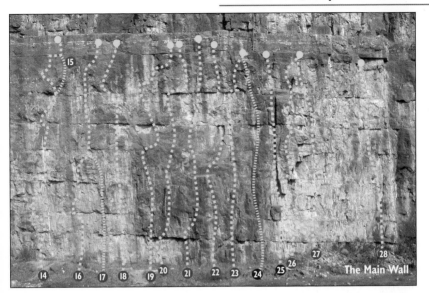

finish up the slab. The original finish crossed the slab rightwards.
Mark Pretty, Ian Jones, 1985 / Gary Gibson, 2003

14 Megalithic Man ★ ★ F6b+

18m The classic of the wall. Varied and sportingly bolted low down, leading to a superb slabby finish. Start via the orange patch; go leftwards through the triangular overlap and rightwards across the upper slab.
Ian French, Chris Wright, Steve France, 1985

15 Megalithic Man Super-Direct ★ ★ F6c+

18m Harder than the original, but with a series of excellent moves. Fingery.
Gary Gibson, 1998

16 Poisonality ★ F7a

18m The direct version of An Ancient Rhythm, again with a well-defined crux section. The line climbs direct to a faint, left-facing corner
Gary Gibson, 1991

17 An Ancient Rhythm ★ F6c+

18m A cruxy lower section past the second bolt runner leads to a pleasantly sustained thin crack above.
Ian French, Chris Wright, Steve France, 1985

18 Demolition Man ★ F7a

18m A typical product of the mid 'eighties. Scantily bolted with a fingery start and a blind finish with plenty of space!
Ian French, Mark Pretty, 1986

A good variation, **Ancient Man**, does the start of Ancient Rhythm then makes bold and committing moves direct to gain the finish of Demolition Man. F7a+, although with its run-out nature, it feels more like E5.

19 Shot Yer Bolt ★ ★ F6b+

18m The long borehole gives the start to an old classic now proving the worse for wear. The crux lies in the scoop and the final 6m.
Steve France, Ian French, Chris Wright, Mark Pretty, 1986

20 Southern Man ★ ★ F7a+

18m Classic fingery face climbing with a bold feel to it. The walls immediately to the right of the bore-

A climber high on
School's Out, F6b (page 35).
Photo: Niall Grimes.

hole give the line, the last 6m the entertainment.
John Godding, Mark Pretty, 1986

21 Nice Face, Shame About the Ledge
F6c

18m Appropriately named. A tricky start, thin slab above the ledge and airy finish via a faint flake give this route.
Steve France, Ian French, Chris Wright, 1985

22 Flatworld ★ F7a
18m A very good eliminate on the right edge of the wall. A trying and powerful crux repels many.
Gary Gibson, 1998

23 Lost Monolith F6b+
18m Easy ledges and a straightforward crack lead to a pleasant crux bulge. Good climbing after a scruffy start.
Ian France, John Godding, Mark Pretty, 1986

24 Sound as a Carp E1 5b
18m The shallow groove leading to bolts higher up.
Anthony Bennett, Chris Goodwin, 2001

25 Spring Awakening HVS 5a
18m A straight thin crack on the right-hand side of the wall gives another good traditional route finishing at an obvious tree.
Senan Hennessy, Ian Smith, 1986

26 Monkey Stole my Walkman ★ F6b
18m The edge of the wall taken via the left-hand side of the striking arête. Looks detached and may well be? A handful of hard moves become even harder when climbed on the arête itself.
Nick Taylor, 2000 / Gary Gibson, 2003

27 Winter Fingers F6b
15m Start 5m right of Monkey Stole my Walkman. Keeping right of the line of bolts provides a tough and solid pitch for the grade. Climbing the corner on the left is loose and is not the route!
Gary Gibson, 2001

28 Mice Breaker F6b+
15m Hollow holds throughout. A direct line up the wall 8m to the right and left of the prominent

groove. Worrying and sportingly bolted but improving with traffic.
Gary Gibson, 2001

Main Wall - Androids Sector

The first section of cliff seen when entering the quarry provides a host of medium-grade sport climbs. The nature of the rock gives mainly vertical wall climbs with the odd crack and groove thrown in for good measure.

The first route lies to the right of the prominent arête and has some mixed ground. It is advisable for the belayer to wear a helmet for the first couple of routes and stand well back, perhaps close to the car?

29 Spectrophotometry E2 5b
15m The long V-shaped groove behind the bushes to the right, peg runner.
Senan Hennessy, Ian Smith, 1986

30 Fifty Bolts to the Gallon F6a+
15m Keep to the arête low down. Higher up, two hard moves gain the belay.
Nadim Siddiqui, Nick Colton (both led), 1998

31 Like Ice, Like Fire E2 5c
15m Good climbing. The faint groove and thin flake to the right have a couple of old bolt runners and require traditional gear. There is no lower-off, so make an abseil descent. Or even walk?
Chris Jackson, Bob Conway, 1986

32 Galening Crack ★ HVS 5a
15m The best traditional route in the quarry but you haven't many to choose from now! The crack in the back of a slim V-groove to the right. The substance in the back of the groove is galena, apparently!
Bill Wintrip, Roy Small, 1986

33 The Rotten Word F6c+
15m Surprisingly tough. The route goes straight up the wall 8m to the right: the route eases after the large ledge.
Gary Gibson, 1999

34 Decayed Dance   **F6c**

15m Easy and relatively insignificant climbing leads to a fine headwall. Start 5m to the right, left of the base of a pillar.
Gary Gibson, 1999

To the right is a large shattered pillar with an old traditional route on its left-hand side (**Order Number 59**, E2 5c).

35 A Right Earful   ★ **F6a**

15m The left wall of the large corner via cracks. The shallow groove above gives a hard finish.
Gary Gibson, E Simpson, R Wheatley, 2001

36 Clean Your Mouth Out   ★ **F6c**

15m The right wall of the prominent corner to the right leads to fine moves above the roof on the headwall.
Gary Gibson, 2001

37 The Dust Bunnies   ★ **F6c+**

15m A direct line up the wall to the right leads to a stopper move on the headwall. Telescopic arms or a contortionist manoeuvre pays dividends.
Gary Gibson, 1998

38 Dalken Shield   ★ **F6b**

15m A much better route, though slightly bolder high up. The vague arête to the right, finishing via a steep headwall.
Bob Conway, Chris Jackson, 1986

39 Hardcore, You Know the Score   **F6b**

15m The polished shallow groove behind the tree leads to a peculiar sequence through an overlap. Always popular, hence the veneer.
Jon Cort, Jim Kelly, 1992

40 The Director's Cut   **F6a+**

15m Pleasant climbing squeezed onto the vague rib to the right. Finish at the belay of Bladerunner.
Gary Gibson, Harold Walmsley, Tim Parkinson, 2003

41 Bladerunner   ★ **F6a+**

15m A super little pitch due to its hint of boldness: three bolt runners in its length. The route takes the wall to the right via an obvious scoop.
Bill Gregory, Dave Gregory, 1986

42 A Serial Affair   **F6b**

15m The first line left of the obvious corner provides a good introduction to the sport climbing hereabouts.
Bruce Goodwin, Dave Gregory, 1996 / Gary Gibson, 1998

43 Do Androids Dream of Electric Sheep   **E2 5c**

15m The corner leads to a rightwards line across the wall. Traditional gear.
Mark Pretty, Ian Jones, 1985

The Main Wall

44 Rage ★ **F6b**

15m A direct line up the centre of wall. Better than its right-hand neighbour.
Gary Gibson, 2001

45 The Running Man **F6b**

15m A good pitch that is becoming less enjoyable due to polish, taking the crack 8m right of the corner. A troublesome overhang at half height gives food for thought.
Jim Kelly, 1991

Around to the right is an obvious open-book corner-line.

46 Willie the Kid **F6a**

18m Not brilliant. The large corner. At the roof traverse a long way right to reach the belay.
Dave Williams, 2001

47 Calamity Jane **F6b**

15m Poor. Climb the left-hand side of the arête forming the right wall of the corner. Stiff in its upper half, overbolted in its lower.
Dave Williams, 2001

48 Jeff Garrett **F6a**

15m The wall right of the prominent arête behind the tree.
Dave Williams, 2001

49 The Dogs **F6b+**

15m The shallow groove and wall above. Avoiding the edge of the wall makes it harder, and artificial.
Dave Williams, 2001

Starting from the base of the slope to the left of the cave is:

50 Derailed **F6b**

12m A short, hard wall left of the cave. A long reach helps as do quick feet.
Gary Gibson, Nick Taylor, 2002

The next obvious feature is a prominent cave at 6m, the site of previous diggings by Geoff Birtles and Tom Proctor. After much excavation (see the pile of dirt underneath), Birtles got deep into the heart of Horseshoe. He was never the same again!

51 Passage of Time **F6b**

12m Easy climbing leads to the cave. The headwall above provides the entertainment.
Jim Kelly, Bob Marks, 1991

Lower Tier - The Toilet Sector

The walls to the right provide a series of routes in the bottom grades. The routes are the result of heavy excavation, so be careful with the holds.

52 The Sewer   **F6a+**
11m A crack-line with a short steep upper section.
Dave Williams, 2003

53 Latrine   **F5**
11m The shallow groove-line is pleasant enough.
Dave Williams, Mark Boulton, 2003

54 Armitage   **F6a**
11m An enjoyable face to the right.
Dave Williams, 2003

55 Shanks   **F6a**
11m The black groove, with hollow holds and plenty of loose ones as well!
Dave Williams, Geoff Middlehurst, 2003

56 Potty   **F6a**
11m A poor route.
Dave Williams, Mark Webster, 2003

57 The Bog   **F6a**
11m A steep start leads to good holds leading up the wall above.
Dave Williams, Geoff Middlehurst, 2003

58 Twyfords   **F6a+**
11m The next route starts via a short groove-line. Again, care with the rock is required.
Dave Williams, Geoff Middlehurst, 2003

59 The Small Room   **F6a+**
11m A tricky little steep start gives way to some hollow holds above.
Dave Williams, Geoff Middlehurst, 2003

60 Thomas Crapper   **F6a**
11m Perhaps the best route in this section, with easy climbing low down and a fine juggy roof finale.
Dave Williams, Geoff Middlehurst, 2003

The final route is situated in the far right-hand corner of the bay.

61 Montezuma's Revenge   **F6a+**
12m A relatively poor route with a hard section at half-height. For the man who has done everything?
David Simmonite, Nadim Siddiqui, 1998

The Upper Tier

A super place to climb without the attendant hordes of the lower tier, and an open gentle atmosphere coupled with a degree of exposure. Although its routes are generally much shorter this section of crag offers something different due its previously mentioned attributes. It is accessed by scrambling up the worn path in the banking, leading to the right side of the walls.

The walls face south, and get afternoon and evening sunshine. They take virtually no seepage.

At the far left-hand side of the tier where it almost merges with the lower tier is a handful of routes.

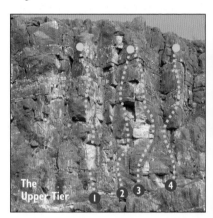

1 The Soggy Bottom Boys   **F6b+**
12m The right-hand side of a slim arête on the end of the tier. A couple of quite testing moves.
Gary Gibson, 2003

2 Man of Constant Sorrow   **F5+**
12m The left-hand side of a bubbly quartz arête starting via a crack.
Gary Gibson, 2003

3 Big Rock Candy Mountain ★ **F6a**
12m The right-hand side of the quartz arête gives an excellent little pitch with plenty of exposure.
Gary Gibson, 2003

4 Everett's Arête   F6a
12m The poor and insignificant arête to the right. One testing move.
Gary Gibson, 2003

5 FOP   F6a
12m An isolated wall 10m to the right. Poor.
Gary Gibson, 2003

The remainder of the routes are situated on the upper tier proper. At its left-hand side is a pleasant-looking wall.

6 No Way is Patience a Virtue   F6b
11m The left-hand side of the wall with a tricky initial wall involving a fingery pull.
Nick Taylor, 2000

7 Oh Brother Where Art Thou?   F6a
10m The route lies on the right-hand side of the wall above a ledge. Good but not as good as the film.
Gary Gibson, 2002

Bolting sport routes

is a hard and time-consuming activity, almost exclusively undertaken at the bolter's own expense, an activity from which all climbers using these crags will benefit. If you feel like contributing to this activity, you can send donations to Gary Gibson, Keristone, Carr Bank, Oakamoor, Staffordshire, which will go directly to the bolt fund.

8 Dapper Dan   ★ F6a
12m The arête to the right. Enjoyable open climbing.
Gary Gibson, Richie Sanderson, 2001

To the right is an area of poor rock with an isolated arête in its centre.

9 The Cretan   F6b+
11m The innocuous-looking arête. Take it mostly on its right-hand side to finish via a thin crack - the groove is not the route.
Gary Gibson, 2001

10 Theseus Saurus   F6b+
11m A short wall to the right leads to an enjoyable few moves on an obvious tower.
Gary Gibson, 2001

11 It's All Greek to Me   F6b
11m The thin crack system direct past a ledge. The start and finish provide the interest.
Gary Gibson, Nick Taylor, 2001

12 The Minor Tour   F6c+
11m A very hard start to the left of the cave finishing via a short technical face. The start can be avoided on the right- The Minor de -Tour F6c.
Gary Gibson, 2001

13 Her Aklion   F6c
9m Innocuously situated above the cave. Thuggy climbing once the start has been overcome.
Gary Gibson, 2001

The Upper Tier

⑭ By Zeus ★ F6a+
12m The pleasant right-hand arête of the tower has hard starting moves leading to an open slab.
Gary Gibson, 2002

⑮ First Pryse F5
12m The slim face to the right starting up a groove.
Dave Williams, 2001

⑯ White Dove ★ E2 5c
12m The thin nut-protected crack.
Chris Wright, Ian French, John Godding, 1986

⑰ Nullo in Mundo Pax Sincera F6c+
12m A hard eliminate requiring a lot of discipline to stick closely to the bolts.
Rehan Siddiqui, Colin Struthers, 1998

⑱ A Liberal Smear F6c+
12m Just that is needed for the crux moves at the top. But off what you may ask?
Gary Gibson, Tim Gallagher, 2001

⑲ Labour Relations ★ F6c+
12m The smooth slab to the right taken centrally to gain the fine overlap and headwall.
Gary Gibson, 2001

⑳ P.M.'s Question Time ★ E3 5c
12m Climb to the left side of the overlap then trend up and right to finish.
Malcolm Taylor, Darren Hawkins, T Goodwin, 1986

㉑ Sir Pryse ★ F6a+
12m Pleasant climbing through the scarred overlap to the right of the prominent pillar.
Dave Williams, Mark Boulton, 2001

㉒ Oy Missus F6c
12m The left-hand side of the slab to the right gives a slippery prize. Hard to avoid the corner on the left. Verging on F6c+.
Gary Gibson, 2001

㉓ Mr Blue Sky ★ F7a
12m Very technical and slippery moves on the right-hand side of the inset slab. Unusual.
Chris Wright, Steve France, 1986

㉔ Smoke Gets in Your Eyes F6b+
12m The short arête 8m to the right is started on its left-hand side. Finish leftwards on the slab.
Steve France, Chris Wright, 1985

㉕ Mumble Jumble ★ ★ F7a+
12m An overhang! All hard moves surround this or do they? Keep to the centre of pillar below to the right of the corner to reach it.
Gary Gibson, 2001

㉖ Fargo F6a+
10m The straight thin crack with a low bulge and awkward finish. You can extend the route by swinging right from the belay to join Blue Sunday.
Gary Gibson, Graham Mason, Nadim Siddiqui, 2001

㉗ Blue Sunday ★ **F6b**

12m The centre of wall starting just to the left of a cave. Pleasantly sustained.
Steve France, Mark Pretty, Chris Wright, Ian French, 1986

㉘ Do It Yourself **F6c**

12m The very hard middle section may require telescopic arms. Keep direct to the line of bolts low down.
Gary Gibson, Nadim Siddiqui, 2001

㉙ Kushti **F6a**

12m The thin crack-line lying 8m to the right. Worthwhile.
Gary Gibson, 2002

㉚ Lovely Bubbly **F6c+**

12m The first line left of the corner. Hard and technical moves at half-height.
Gary Gibson, 2002

Ten metres to the right again is the isolated pitch of:

㉛ Slam the Jam **F5**

12m Prominent groove and jamming crack above. Keep to right wall lower down.
Gary Gibson, Nick Taylor, 2003

㉜ Nijinski **E2 5b**

11m The slim, slabby face on the left. Move left and then up from half height. Direct is 5c.
Darren Hawkins, Malcolm Taylor, 1985

㉝ The Party Animal **F6b**

9m The left arête taken on its right-hand side at the top. Climbing the left-hand side of the arête gives a F5+.
Mark Pretty, Sean Coffey, John Godding, 1986

㉞ Café Bleu ★ **E3 5c**

10m A little gem up the centre of the face. Tiny wires protect the start.
Malcolm Taylor, Darren Hawkins, 1985

㉟ Dinky Toy **E4 6a**

11m A short pitch on the right-hand side of the wall has two old peg runners.
Nigel Slater, P Grant, 1986

Upper Left-Hand Walls

These are a collection of walls facing the Upper Tier, and on the same level. They are accessed by walking up the big ramp opposite the Main Wall. The first sector encountered is surprisingly small.

The Tiny Tier

One of the world's smallest pieces of rock sits just above the access ramp. There are 2 routes on it.

① A Tracky Little Problem **F4**
4m The little left line.
Mike & Luke Hunt, 2001

② A Tracky Little Bleeder **F5**
4m The little right line.
Luke & Mike Hunt, 2001

Star Trek Wall

This is the long grey wall which lies a little further along the tier, containing a number of easier sport climbs of limited quality.

The wall faces east and gets sunshine only in the early morning.

3 **Gargle Blaster**   **F6a**
6m The short tricky wall on the left-hand side of the face.
Mike Hunt, Jane Livingstone, 2001

4 **Uranus**   **F3**
8m The left-hand of two crack-lines, sharing bolts with the next route.
Mike Hunt, Luke Hunt, 2001

Left: Kushti, F6a, one of the many fine climbs on the rarely-visited Upper Tier of Horseshoe Quarry (page 45).
Photo: Niall Grimes.

5 **Luke Skywalker**   **F4**
8m The right-hand crack.
Mike Hunt, 2001

6 **Klingon**   **F4**
8m Another faint crack-line.
Mike Hunt, 2001

7 **Saturn's Ring**   **F5**
8m The wall to the right.
Mike Hunt, 2001

8 **Vogon**   ★ **F6a**
7m The star denotes the best route on this wall, not comparisons elsewhere.
Mike Hunt, 2001

9 **Dr Who?**   **F6a+**
7m Pass a prominent scar by hard moves.
Gary Gibson, 2001

10 **Beam me Across Scotty**   **F5**
12m Traverse the wall from right to left, clipping as many bolts on the other routes as possible, to boldly lower off Gargle Blaster.
Bruce Goodwin, Tina Priestley, 2003

The Upper Bay

The next two routes are situated on a small wall to the right of the Star Trek wall. The stumps of a butchered elderberry tree marks the wall.

⑪ Taking Liberties   **F6c+**
8m   The centre of the wall leads to a very hard finish. Good.
Gary Gibson, 2001

⑫ Statuesque   **F6a+**
8m   The thin crack system on the right-hand side of the wall. Again worthwhile.
Gary Gibson, 2001

The final routes are on the arête and corner just across the bay.

⑬ Mucker's Wall   **F6a**
10m   The slabby wall left of Citizen's Edge.
Gary Gibson, 2001

⑭ Citizen's Edge   **F4**
10m   The innocuous arête in the centre of the bay.
Dave Williams, 2001

The last routes are based around the right arête of the bay.

⑮ The Whinger   **F6a+**
12m   The right-hand side of the prominent arête on the right-hand side of the bay. A poor addition.
Dave Williams, 2001

⑯ Off Limits   **F6a**
12m   From the ledge, climb the centre of the narrow wall right of the arête via the thin crack.
Dave Williams, 2001

Neil Foster on Rain Dance, F6c, one of the older classics to be found at Horseshoe. (page 35). Photo: Niall Grimes.

The Matlock Area 2

Pete Cresswell on Sample the
Mantel, F7b, at Lorry Park Quarry
(page 73). Photo: Tim Cresswell.

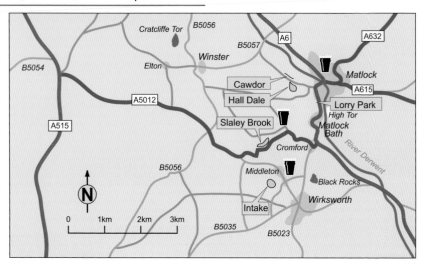

Hall Dale Quarry

O.S. Ref. **SK288600**   Altitude: **140m a.s.l.**

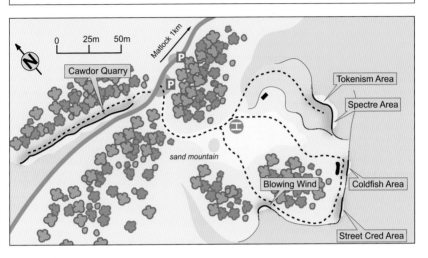

A truly surprising find, this vast quarry has yielded a number of excellent routes, as good as any of their grade in the Peak. These are mainly concentrated around a right-angled bay towards the back of the quarry, although there are also several other small pockets of climbing on surrounding outcrops of good rock, each with its own character.

The climbing
Almost 30 routes, with a good equal spread from F6a to F7a+. These are all single-pitch climbs, up to 20m high, and well-bolted. The main area has routes that climb steep walls and bold features (the Tokenism Walls), and routes up the very steep slab on the wall to the right, which is capped by a big overhang (the Spectre Walls).

Conditions & aspect
The main section is open and quick-drying, and takes very little seepage. However, as only the Tokenism area gets significant amounts of sunshine, it is best enjoyed on warmer days. The other areas are also very quick-drying, but again, only get a lit-

tle sunshine in the evening. As such, it is probably best visited in the summer.

Parking & approach
From the south side of the bridge in Matlock, take the first right into Snitterton Lane, just after the station, and drive straight up the hill. After 400m the hill levels out. Continue along this road for a further 400m to a lay-by on the left-hand side of the road, the entrance to Hall Dale Quarry, and park. Enter the quarry, and orientate yourself by the large helicopter landing-pad located after a couple of hundred metres. **Walk-in:** All under 10 minutes.

Layout
This is a massive quarry with a lot of fragmented rock. The lower and upper tiers are generally poor, although the right-hand side of the quarry does offer some worthwhile sections of rock. The main interest of the quarry lies in the bay at the right-hand side of the middle tier, itself terminated by a large boulder-strewn slope - the term scree slope here would certainly be an understatement!

The Tokenism Walls

The Main Area

To reach this area, two large walls at right-angles to each other up at the back of the middle quarry, follow the track into the quarry to arrive at the helicopter pad. Turn left at the helicopter pad and follow the track around and above the lower tier, rightwards to the final bay and two distinct walls.

The Tokenism Walls

The first walls encountered on entering the bay, these lie at right angles to the Spectre Wall and offer an unusual style of climbing, some with fossil-encrusted rock. Features here include a towering right-hand wall, orange in its lower half, a slim wall to its left and a central wall of compact rock. On the fringes of the wall, obvious when you approach the face, are two good sections of rock harbouring one route each.

The wall faces south-west and receives the sun from 2pm onwards; it takes no seepage and dries very quickly.

When entering the main area of cliff, two routes, not shown on the topo, are evident at the entrance to this section of crag and lie just right of a massive boulder slope.

① Hide and Peek ★ **F7a**

18m An orange-flecked wall in the first bay has a hard starting section. The arête above makes this worthwhile.
Gary Gibson, 2000

② Opening Call **F5**

18m This white wall is situated 30m to the right of the initial bay and just to the right of a prominent detached pillar. An easy wall leads to a ledge. The white face above is pleasant.
Gary Gibson, Tim Gallagher, 2002

The main bulk of routes in this area lie 60m to the right.

③ Dinnertime Special **F6a**

18m The easier left-hand line. Keep to the face where possible. Warning: not repeated since the demise of a large flake.
Gary Gibson, 2002

④ Tokenism ★ **F6b**

18m The centre of the face. Increasingly technical moves lead to a tricky finale.
Gary Gibson, 2000

The Spectre Wall

5 Trotskyism ★ F7a

18m A problematic start on the lower arête leads to good face climbing above.
Gary Gibson, 2002

6 Beamsplitter F7a

20m The slender overlapped wall. Hardest on the headwall and unnerving through the roofs.
Gary Gibson, 2002

7 The Crinoid Smile ★ F6c+

20m Very unusual rock, especially higher up. The lower wall is easier, though a tad dusty. The wall above the half-height ledge provides the interest, both in morphology and difficulty.
Gary Gibson, 2002

8 A Fossil on Fossils ★ F6c

20m An easier lower section leads to good climbing above the angled flake-line. Unusual fossilised rock.
Gary Gibson, 2002

The Spectre Wall

The Spectre Walls are the centrepiece of the quarry, offering some very fine climbing with a variety not normally associated with quarries. The approach climbing to and above the central roof is generally on immaculate rock. On the right-hand side of the wall is a fine black slab with a couple of easier routes, the right-hand of which can suffer the effects of 'wash-down'.

The wall faces in a north-westerly direction and gets sunshine after 4pm. It can remain damp, dark and dismal in the winter months but is an ideal summer venue.

9 Ghost Story F6b+

20m The vague slender pillar on the left-hand side of the face. Can be a little dirty.
Gary Gibson, 2000

10 Lick Yours F7a

20m Hardest through the roof: some hollow blocks exist hereabouts. Excellent above.
Gary Gibson, 2001

11 Spooktakula ★ ★ F7a+

20m Hard moves through the centre of the roof, where long arms and a short body pay dividends, are complemented by delicate face climbing above and below.
Gary Gibson, 2000

⑫ **Southern Discomfort** ★ ★ **F6c+**

20m A great pitch slap bang through the roof system giving the crux. Fine face climbing above and below.
Gary Gibson, Dave Law, 2000

⑬ **Burning Spirits** ★ ★ **F6b+**

20m Similar in character to The Spectre and just as fine. Hardest through the stepped roof.
Gary Gibson, 2000

⑭ **The Dark Side of the Room** ★ **F7a+**

20m A direct assault on the double-tiered overhangs in the upper part of the face. The top roof provides the difficulties where a long reach helps. The walls below provide easier climbing.
Gary Gibson, 2000

⑮ **The Spectre** ★ ★ **F6b+**

20m The classic of the face. Slabby walls to a hanging arête and wide jam crack in a great situation.
Gary Gibson, Dave Law, 2000

⑯ **God is Good** ★ ★ **F6c**

20m A fine delicate pitch angling rightwards across the lip of the wall. Difficulties are centred in the first 12m.
Gary Gibson, 2000

⑰ **Unblackened** ★ **F6a**

15m A good warm-up taking the left-hand arête and slab. Tricky only at the start.
Gary & Hazel Gibson, 2000

⑱ **First and Last** **HVS 5a**

15m The thin crack splitting the black slab to a lower off on the left.
Nick Taylor, Andy Beaumont, 1999

⑲ **Black Helicopter Ride** **F6a**

15m The centre of the black slab. Good rock, although it can be dusty.
Nick Taylor, Andy Beaumont, 2000

The Lower Quarry

Situated in the lower quarry are a number of smaller sections, each giving up a handful of decent pitches, and each with its own character.

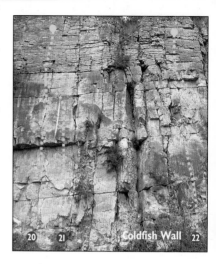

Coldfish Wall

This is a tall, white wall of good rough rock, rising just behind a dark hole in the quarry floor. The wall was named after a food wrapper found at the bottom of the cliff.

The wall faces west, dries very quickly and receives little sunshine until late on in the evening.

⑳ **The Coldfish** ★ **F7a+**

20m A fine route with a good long feel to it. The thin central crack-system leads onto the upper wall. Hard and sustained climbing leads to a good ledge, giving access to easier climbing above.
Gary Gibson, 2002

㉑ **Gutted** **F7b+**

20m This route is based around the desperate thin crack and overlap on the right-hand side of the compact white wall. Move left to join The Coldfish from the ledge.
Gary Gibson, 2002

㉒ **Vertical Fish** **F6c**

20m A long and pleasantly sustained pitch up a thin white pillar. One or two hollow holds but it should clean up with traffic.
Gary Gibson, 2002

Paul Harrison on Burning
Spirits. F6b+
(opposite page).
Photo: David Simmonite.

Street Cred

Street Cred

This section of wall is to be found in the top right-hand corner of the quarry and is easily identified by its orange colouring.

The wall faces north and gains only a fragment of sunshine in the morning and evening. It takes little seepage and dries quickly. A good venue for very hot summer days.

㉓ Cycle Path   **F6a+**
15m This lies above a pinnacle to the left. Juggy walls lead to the upper left-hand arête.
Gary Gibson, Gordon Jenkin, 2002

㉔ Totally Street Cred   ★ **F6c+**
15m The centre of the orange wall gives a fine sustained pitch, although still a tad dusty.
Gary Gibson, Gordon Jenkin, 2002

㉕ Road Rage   **F6c+**
11m A hard finger-crack above a lower, wider crack. Surprisingly tough.
Gary Gibson, 2002

㉖ Cry on My Hard Shoulder   ★ **F5+**
12m An enjoyable arête, which is hardest through the left-hand side of the large overlap.
Gary & Hazel Gibson, Gordon Jenkin, 2002

Blowing Wind

Blowing Wind

Named after a successful wager on a Grand National horse, these walls are to be found on the right-hand side of the lower bowl of the quarry, on a promontory. On entry to the quarry, locate the helicopter-landing pad and take a 90-degree right turn. Walk through a 'gap' in the embankment to locate this short wall above a beautifully green pasture.

The wall receives morning sunshine until 11.30am in the summer months and takes seepage only during the winter months.

㉗ Guff it and See   **F6c**
12m The hardest route on the wall up its left-hand side. Keep direct on the line.
Gary Gibson, 2002

㉘ Blowing Wind   **F6b**
12m The centre of the wall has an awkward start and finish. The best route hereabouts.
Gary Gibson, Gordon Jenkin, 2002

㉙ Backdraught   **F6b**
12m A short wall leads to a groove and tricky finish leftwards.
Gary Gibson, Gordon Jenkin, 2002

Paul Harrison on The
Spectre, F6b+ (page 56).
Photo: David Simmonite.

Cawdor Quarry

O.S. Ref. **SK288604** | Altitude: **130m a.s.l.**

An interesting little find with ease of access, on generally good rock and with plenty of routes in the low to middle grades. Some of the routes still contain loose holds but these are slowly cleaning up to make the cliff well worth a visit. A large concentration of routes makes it an ideal place to tick off lots of climbs in a short visit. It can also be combined with a visit to Hall Dale Quarry, just across the road.

Parking & approach

Park in the entrance to Hall Dale Quarry (see Hall Dale approach). Cross to the opposite side of the road, hop over the wall by a sign for Matlock and descend the slope. **Walk-in**: From 1 to 5 minutes.

The climbing

Over 60 routes, nearly all in the F6 range, with only a handful that are harder or easier. All single-pitch, from 10m to 25m. The climbs often follow good features, with plenty of walls, arêtes and cracks to give the climbs lots of character. The rock is not as solid as on some cliffs, although most of the longer-established routes are now fairly solid.

Situation & aspect

A dark cliff, which is thickly lined with trees at its base and faces north, receiving very little sunshine except in the early or late hours of the summer. For this reason it is best visited in the summer. It can become damp after rain, although, when dry, the cliff provides a superb spot to tick a number of routes in a day or is similarly ideal for a short evening's visit.

Boffin Wall

The first section of cliff has an indistinct feel to it, with areas of relatively uninteresting rock. In between the odd worthwhile route does exist / has been excavated. The first routes lie just at the bottom of the descent slope.

1 Slug Matador   **F6a**
10m The first wall at the bottom of the slope, up a tiny groove moving right to the belay of the next route.
Nick Taylor, Pete Clark, 2003

2 Boffin   **F6c+**
10m The first compact wall at the bottom of the slope gives a fingery face climb with the crux at the start.
Nick Taylor, Tim Parkinson, Ian Smith, 2000

3 Nit-Wit   **F4**
10m The straight crack-line right of the smooth starting wall. Move left to belay.
Nick Taylor, Pete Clark, 2003

4 Pedal to the Metal   **F6a+**
10m A tricky starting wall leads to easy ground and a steep and reachy finale.
Gary Gibson, 2003

5 All in Glory   ★ **F6c**
12m Eight metres to the right lies this innocuous faint rib. Fine rock and good climbing, with a few fingery moves.
Gary Gibson, Mark Richardson, Phil Gibson, 2003

6 Thirst for Glory   **F6a**
12m More pleasant climbing to the right, via a slab, shallow groove and steep finish.
Gary Gibson, 2003

7 Woodward on the Wing   **F6a**
12m A vague blunt arête and short wall lead to a ledge.
Nick Taylor, 2003

8 Empo on a Spring   **F6a+**
12m The pleasant short corner and easier wall above, featuring a few stiff pulls. Alternatively, swing left from the corner to continue boldly up the centre of the wall (**Alan on a String**, F6b, Nick Taylor, 2003).
Nick Taylor, 2003

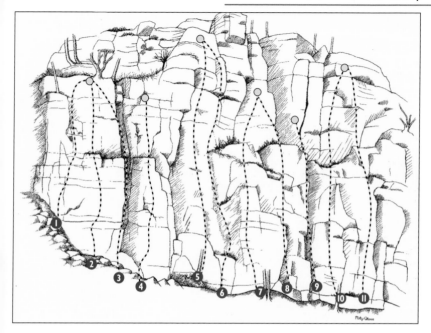

9 Footsie F6a+
12m A sharp arête ends all too briefly. Easy then to the ledge.
Gary Gibson, 2003

10 Unbalanced F5
12m Sweet climbing taking a faint rib and short steep headwall.
Gary Gibson 2003

11 Taylor Made F6b+
12m From a ledge, a steep start on edges and crimps leads to easier climbing above.
Gary Gibson, 2003

The next series of routes marks the start of the cliff proper and lies about 10m further on. The first route begins behind a large tree.

12 Ta Nick F7a
15m A straightforward wall leads to a technical face on hidden holds where a long reach helps.
Gary Gibson, 2003

13 Lady Luck F6a+
18m From just to the left of the arête, trend leftwards up the face finishing via a crack-line.
Gary & Phil Gibson, 2003

14 Apologia ★ F6a
18m The excellent sharp arête leads to a steep wall on good hidden holds.
Gary & Phil Gibson, Mark Richardson, 2003

Encore Wall

The first main bulk of the cliff is centred on two walls of excellent compact limestone, with steep walls and grooves. These have been well-trodden and the routes have improved because of it.

15 Rust Never Sleeps ★ F6b+
18m Follow a wide crack until a step right to the third bolt is followed by fine sustained climbing above.
Gary Gibson, 2003

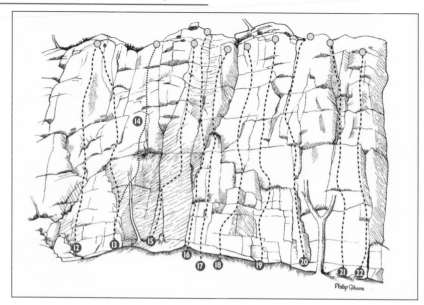

16 **Willows Never Weep** ★ **F6a+**

18m The main angle of the bay, followed in its entirety, gives a good sustained pitch. Some creaky holds low down but all close to the bolts.
Gary Gibson, 2003

17 **Trust Never Keeps** **F6c**

15m Just right again. Easy climbing up a rib leads to a steep and fingery climax on the headwall.
Gary Gibson, 2003

18 **Encore Plus** **F6b**

18m The left-hand line saves its best till last.
Gary & Phil Gibson, Mark Richardson, 2003

19 **The Impulsive, Compulsive Beat** **F6b+**

18m The right-hand line, after a ledgy start, is a far better proposition than the last climb. A good sustained pitch with no identifiable crux.
Gary & Phil Gibson, Nick Taylor, 2003

20 **Triple X** ★ **F6a+**

15m The superb steep crack-line to the right with a short hard section. Exit right to the belay.
Gary Gibson, 2003

21 **New Face in Hell** **F6c**

15m A very technical little wall gives access to easier and more pleasant climbing up a prominent groove-line.
Nick Taylor, Gary Gibson, 2003

22 **Coward** ★ **F6a+**

18m The right arête of the next wall leads to a sharp groove and pleasant open arête.
Nick Taylor, 2000

23 **Family Ties** ★ **F6a+**

20m The prominent corner-line gives a sustained route, far harder than its appearance might suggest.
Gary & Phil Gibson, 2003

24 **Freaky Friday** ★ **F6a+**

20m Again worthwhile. The steep wall and face lead past a groove to a flourishing finale.
Gary Gibson, 2003

25 **Cawdor Nothing** ★ ★ **F6c+**

20m Climb the straightforward face to the right. The final wall provides a short technical section and all-out finish. Excellent.
Gary & Phil Gibson, 2003

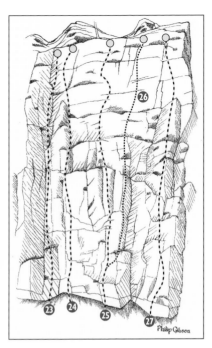

26 The Cutting Crew ★ F7a
20m The right-hand side of the impressive headwall provides a marginally tougher and more fingery proposition than the last climb.
Gary & Phil Gibson, 2003

27 Virgin on Porn F6b+
10m Climb the innocuous short rib to gain a ledge and final sharp arête. A poor route requiring more cleaning.
Gary Gibson, 2003

Porn Walls

The slightly inset walls to the right provide a number of easier grade sport routes. Some of these do have a damp start due to a spring emanating from the foot of the cliff but this is easily overcome in favour of the fine grey rock above. The wall gained its name from a pile of rude magazines found at the foot of the cliff.

28 Boobie Prize ★ F6a+
20m The first line to the right of the corner has a distinct crux just above half-height. A long reach may help as does a determined approach.
Gary & Hazel Gibson, 2003

29 Breast Stroke F6a+
18m A little hollow. The snaking crack and groove lines prove surprisingly tricky in places.
Gary Gibson, 2003

30 Breast is Best ★ F6a
20m Perhaps the best route on the wall. A short wall and vague grey rib lead to a rightwards exit. Pleasantly sustained.
Gary, Hazel & Phil Gibson, 2003

31 Porn to Run F6a+
20m The next line to the right has a definite crux where a long reach is an advantage.
Gary, Hazel & Phil Gibson, 2003

32 The Porn Curtain F5+
20m Another long crack-line gives the easiest pitch on the wall. Good climbing after a hollow, damp start. More cleaning may be required here.
Gary & Phil Gibson, 2003

33 Porn Palace ★ F6b+
20m Start as for the Porn Curtain but continue direct to a fine climactic headwall. Airy.
Gary & Phil Gibson, 2003

34 Vibrators F6a+
18m The final line of the wall, taking a faint groove. Only for use when nothing else may be available.
Gary Gibson, 2003

The walls now stand forward again with three distinct sections in the form of three pillars. The routes here are on excellent rock throughout.

35 Brazilian Style ★ ★ F6c+
20m Superb, sustained climbing on fine grey rock. The left-hand arête of the first pillar gives a fine introduction to the more technical routes hereabouts.
Gary Gibson, Mark Richardson, 2003

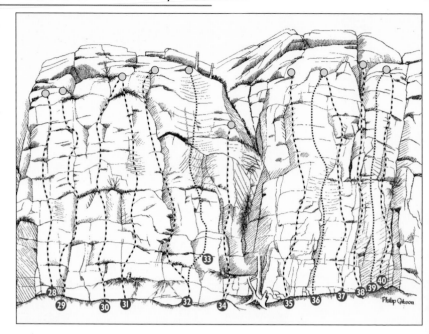

36 All Mine ★ ★ F6c+

20m Very worthwhile but much more airy than the last climb. The centre of the pillar started from a flake gives excellent rock, with hidden holds in places. Finish directly to the belay.
Gary Gibson, 2003

37 Yours Truly ★ ★ F6b

20m Superb sustained wall climbing to the left of the prominent fault-line. No hard moves, but it feels quite long.
Pete Clark, Gary Gibson, Nick Taylor, 2003

38 Analyse This F6b

20m The steep and strenuous fault-line gives an impressive pitch for the grade. Lots of good holds but can you hang on?
Pete Clark, Gary Gibson, Nick Taylor, 2003

39 Demon ★ ★ F6c+

20m The centre of the next pillar gives a fine pitch on excellent rock with generally good holds.
Nick Taylor, Sean McCloughlin, 2000

40 Weakling ★ F6b

20m The right-hand side of the face via a flake and short shallow groove.
Nick Taylor, 2000

Fisherman Wall

The next series of walls is long and complex and features a number of lengthy routes on the best sections of rock. The wall extends as far as a fence which marks the edge of a large pool, the preserve of the fisherman. No climbing exists beyond this fence in order that both the fisherman and the climbers can follow their sport in peace. The first routes begin 20m right of the last climbs at a short narrow platform. Please respect this.

41 Dirty Duck F6a

18m The left of three lines gives surprisingly pleasant climbing on good holds and using a crucial calcite pocket.
Nick Taylor, Gary Gibson, 2003

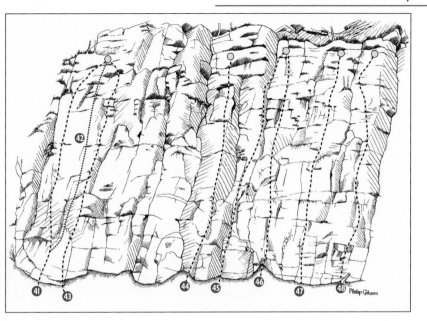

42 Giddy Ant   **F6b**

18m The left-hand of two lines via a faint rib. A short crux section at mid-height is followed by some good climbing.
Nick Taylor, Gary Gibson, 2003

43 Chocopotamus   ★ **F6a+**

18m The right-hand line gives a better route with more consistent moves and fluent climbing.
Nick Taylor, Gary Gibson, 2003

Just right is a strikingly sharp arête and large corner.

44 Fisherman's Friend   ★ **F7a**

22m The arête taken on its left-hand side all the way to a ledge gives fingery and technical climbing. The final moves, attacking a smooth-looking headwall, give the crux and require a massive reach.
Gary Gibson, 2003

45 Simply Carp   ★ **F6a**

25m The long corner line, exiting right and up via a satisfying steep crack. Pleasant.
Pete Clark, Gary Gibson, 2003

46 On Higher Perches   **F6a+**

22m Start 5m right of the corner and climb the obvious direct line up a vague pillar. A short, tricky section at mid-height provides the interest.
Gary Gibson, Nick Taylor, 2003

47 Pier Review   ★ **F6b+**

22m A fine little route still, unfortunately, with the odd brittle hold. The line centres around a vague pillar of rock 8m to the right. Take this direct with sustained interest.
Gary Gibson, Nick Taylor, 2003

48 High Tench On   **F6c**

22m Difficulties revolve around a crux sequence at the top of the pitch. The wall and vague left arête of the groove provides the route.
Gary Gibson, Nick Taylor, 2003

49 Ma Pechere   ★ **F5**

25m The long corner-line gives a pitch of varied interest for the grade. Move right at the top to gain the belay.
Gary Gibson, Nick Taylor, 2003

Alan Taylor on Coward, F6a+ (page 63).
Photo: Nick Taylor.

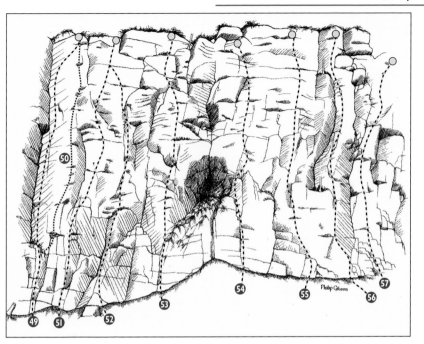

50 Poached Please ★ **F6a+**
25m Very enjoyable climbing. This route tackles the right-hand arête of the groove-line by a series of varied moves.
Gary Gibson, Nick Taylor, 2003

51 The Fish Course **F6c**
25m A thin crack on the left-hand side of a vague arête gains a short steep wall with good moves and a tricky finale.
Gary Gibson, 2003

52 Of Course, the Fish **F6b+**
25m A shallow groove and steep, faint, left-facing groove leads to the same tricky finale as the last route.
Gary Gibson, 2003

53 Carpin' About **F6b**
22m The next line 6m to the right. A prominent cave at half height is passed to the left.
Gary Gibson, 2003

54 Scales of Justice ★ **F6a+**
22m Good climbing starting up a vague rib and climbing the wall to the right of the cave.
Gary Gibson, 2003

55 Gone Fishing **F6c**
25m This climb is centred around a smooth-looking headwall at 12m. This route gains it direct and finishes via a short wall. Interest is maintained throughout.
Gary Gibson, 2003

56 Hook, Line and Sinker **F6b**
25m A varied climb snaking up the slim groove-lines to the right. Gain this by a tricky move on the lower arête.
Gary Gibson, 2003

57 Small Fry **F6a+**
22m Five metres right again. Climb the vague pillar between grooves exiting rightwards to a belay.
Gary Gibson, 2003

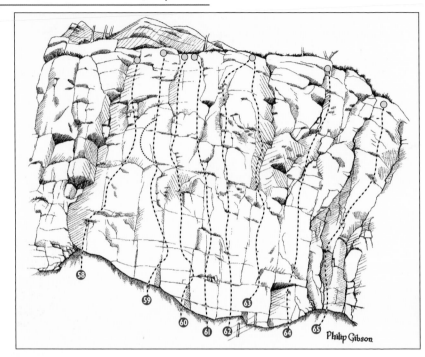

Philip Gibson

58 Payback ★ ★ F6c+

25m An intricate lower wall gives access to a slim corner and excellent headwall.
Gary Gibson, Pete Clark, 2003

59 Totally Wired ★ ★ F7a+

25m The centre of the wall. A tricky start gains a ledge. A desperate sequence above or a detour to the left at F6c (**Just Step S'ways**, Nick Taylor, 2003) gains the superb finishing wall.
Nick Taylor, Gary Gibson, 2003

60 Spectre vs. Rector ★ F6b+

25m A short tricky wall and a thin crack (requiring a long reach) gain a vague groove high up.
Nick Taylor, Gary Gibson, 2003

61 Agony Ant ★ F6b

25m A tricky overlap start followed by fine climbing via shallow grooves and a prominent finishing flake.
Pete Clark, Gary Gibson, Nick Taylor, 2003

62 Flaked Out ★ F6a+

25m The wall via a shallow scoop to a finish via the prominent flake crack. Good climbing.
Pete Clark, Gary Gibson, 2003

63 Dog Canute ★ F6b

22m This lies above the fence. An intricate rib leads with a difficult move to a flake. Finish up the left wall of this. Again, very worthwhile.
Nick Taylor, Gary Gibson, Pete Clark, 2003

64 Feeding Frenzy ★ ★ F6b

22m Around the corner. A superb route taking the slim, sustained wall on positive holds to an impressive finish for the grade.
Pete Clark, Gary Gibson, Nick Taylor, 2003

65 Fisherman's Finale F6c

18m The final pillar just right followed by the arête with a suitably tricky finale!
Pete Clark, Gary Gibson, 2003

Lorry Park Quarry

O.S. Ref. **SK297597**   Altitude: **140m a.s.l.**

by Pete Cresswell

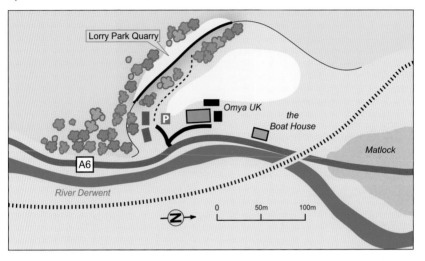

Lorry Park Quarry lies just on the outskirts of Matlock, giving a small concentration of difficult sport climbs on slightly overhanging walls, and a handful of very well-formed crack climbs. It is set in the grounds of the old Tarmac offices which leaves it with a somewhat earthy ambience, although trees do allow the climber to ignore this somewhat.

The climbing

There are 11 sport routes here, all taking tall and fairly featureless walls. As such, the climbs are fingery and technical. Most of these routes are in the F7 range. There are also a number of perfectly-formed finger-cracks and the amazing stepped corner of On The Road which, if it were anywhere else, would be one of the classics of the Peak.

Conditions & aspect

This is a very shady crag, getting only a little sun in the early morning in summer. The routes are very

clean, although not all the rock is perfect, and some scrunching can occur. Some of the cracks seep a little after a downpour, although it can also be fairly sheltered during the rain. A good crag for a hot summer. The setting is not very inspiring, however.

Parking & approach

Coming out of Matlock travelling south, pass under a railway bridge, then the Boat House pub on the right. One hundred metres after this, a sign indicates the entrance to Omya UK. Go in here, and turn immediately left and park. The muddy track ahead leads to ground below the crag. Please be courteous to any residents here, either official or non-official. **Walk-in:** 2 minutes.

Traditional climbs

The quarry is home to a number of stout crack routes which are all noted in the text.

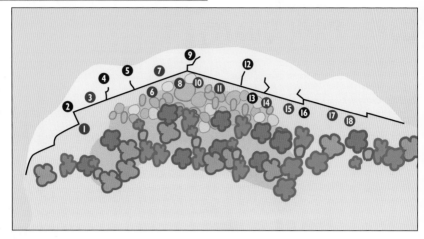

The climbing is based on the long flat wall bounded on its left by a stepped corner. The first route starts on the left arête of this corner.

① Wild Strawberries ★ F6c

28m The bolted arête. Climb the short corner, and continue to the roof. Swing left here (trying not to think about the block the third bolt is in) and carry on up and right to an exposed finish.
Cathy Cresswell, 1996

② On The Road ★★★ E3 5c

28m The impressive double stepped overhang is the classic of the crag, with sustained, well-protected climbing all the way.
Dominic & Daniel Lee, 1981

③ Squealer ★★ F7c

25m The bolted line right of the corner with sustained fingery moves leading to a jug. From here follow the shallow groove to the break before more hard moves lead to a balancey finish. An earlier, indirect version gained the jug from the next crack at F7b+.
Pete Cresswell, 1998

④ Supercrack ★★ E5 6b

25m The crack to the right is sustained and fingery. There is an old peg where the route kinks right, but don't rely on this for the hard top section.
Dominic & Daniel Lee, 1981

⑤ Edge of Darkness E2 5c

23m The next crack. The thrilling finish, up suspect blocks and dubious rock can be avoided by lowering off the twin bolts on the left wall,
Dominic & Daniel Lee, 1981

⑥ Big Spider, Small Bath F7b+

20m The thin crack just right is sustained, taxing, and has a worrying finish.
Pete Cresswell, 1996

⑦ Good Time Emporium ★ F7b

18m A hard start leads to a balancey groove and a reachy finish.
Pete Cresswell, 1996

⑧ Shore Leave F7a

18m Climb the very shallow groove moving right then back left, avoiding Shattered Air.
Pete Cresswell, 1996

⑨ Shattered Air E3 5c

16m The sharp flake crack is poorly-protected. Traverse right and finish as for Deceptive.
Dominic & Daniel Lee, 1981

⑩ Deceptive ★★ F7b

16m As the name suggests, the two thin cracks are harder than they appear.
Pete Cresswell, 1996

Pete Cresswell on Squealer
Indirect, F7b+ (page 70).
Photo: Tim Cresswell.

Cathy Cresswell on the first
ascent of Wild Strawberries,
F6c (page 70).
Photo: Tim Cresswell.

⑪ Project

⑫ Thunder Road ★ **E3 5c**

20m Ascend the crack to the terrace and lower off.
Daniel & Dominic Lee, 1981

⑬ Hell's Angels ★ **E5 6b**

22m Make hard moves off a flake to reach pockets. Carry on to join and finish up Desolation Angels.
Daniel & Dominic Lee, 1981

⑭ Sample the Mantel ★ ★ **F7b**

22m Ascend the blunt rib with difficulty. Cross the traverse line of Desolation Angel and continue to a mantelshelf finish.
Pete Cresswell, 1996

⑮ Baron Samedi ★ **F7b**

21m To the right, climb the wall to the break. Carry on directly to a very shallow groove which is followed to desperate finishing moves.
Pete Cresswell, 1996

⑯ Desolation Angels **E4 6b**

28m Follow the left-trending line which gradually becomes harder. A step left leads to the final crux moves.
Daniel & Dominic Lee, 1981

⑰ Game On ★ **F7a**

10m The short wall has fine moves.
Nadim Siddiqui, Percy Bishton, David Simmonite, 1988

⑱ Go Your Own Way ★ **F7b**

10m The right-hand line is enjoyable.
Nadim Siddiqui, Percy Bishton, David Simmonite, 1988

Slaley Brook

O.S. Ref. **SK275572**   Altitude: **180m a.s.l.**

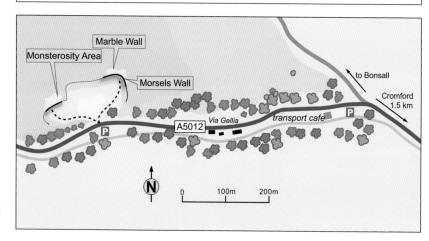

This huge quarry presents a variety of faces with the largest section of rock providing the longest single sport pitch in Britain at 45m, and the right-hand, Marble Walls, providing a number of shorter more accessible pitches with a less intimidating nature.

On entry to the quarry the faces provide a massive, shambling appearance. On closer inspection there are clearly a number of walls of merit. In the top right-hand corner of the quarry is an excellent calcite face, the Marble Walls - the limestone alternative to the Stanage version - with a selection of excellent face climbs on unusual flowstone. The left-hand side of the quarry is the complete antithesis of its neighbour. Huge by contrast, up to 60m in height, with a number of long pitches, unusual by Peak standards and of particular merit being Orangeman, In the End and Too Monsterosity.

The climbing
Forty routes, evenly distributed between F6a and F7b, all single pitch from 12m to a massive 45m in length! All quite steep, with some fingery and some being juggy.

Parking & approach
Either park on the road outside the entrance to the quarry, on a well-used lay-by, or in the larger lay-by 500m towards Matlock, made even more attractive on weekdays when a fine portakabin café serves good fried food and brews. **All walk-ins:** 5 minutes.

Conditions & aspect
Almost all the walls face south and get loads of sun. The left-hand cliffs do suffer one major problem, that of dust. After wash-down the routes can be particularly dusty but for the most part remain clean except for the ledges. A quick abseil descent or waiting for a dry week will probably sort this out. Also, as some of the walls seep a little, it is best to visit in the summer.

Note: Major restabilisation work has been taking place at this quarry at the time of writing. This has not been on the climbing walls themselves, but how it will effect long-term access to the crag remains to be seen.

Tango Walls

Tango Walls

Situated in the top left-hand corner of the quarry, these impressive walls form the left side of the crag, easily identified by their orange nature and a series of striking thin cracks in the upper headwalls. They offer a number of technical face climbs with the occasional crack and arête thrown in for good measure. The arête on the left provides the first route and the remainder are described rightwards from this. Some routes can suffer from dust and these have been noted in the descriptions.

The walls reach a height of 25m, face in a southerly direction getting sunshine all day.

① You've Been Tangoed ★ F7a+
12m The arête contains a right-facing flake. Gaining this via the roof provides the crux, the flake requiring an assertive approach.
Gary Gibson, 2000

② Orange Rising ★ F7a
12m A short wall just right leads to a break. Above this a faint flake gives a precarious mantelshelf and intriguing finish.
Gary Gibson, 2000

③ Repealed F7b
12m Hard. A short wall 8m right of the edge of the wall leads to a ledge. The steep wall above has a memorable finish.
Gary Gibson, 2000

④ Unpealed ★ F7a+
20m Fine climbing with a particularly tantalising finale. The short wall and pocketed slab provides an intricate and insecure start. The headwall provides fine technicalities to the final, crux moves. Can be dusty.
Gary Gibson, 2000

⑤ The Orangeman ★ ★ F6c+
22m A classic of its type taking the sinuous crack in

Streaming & Monsterosity Walls

the slab to the right, to reach a steep and easier finish. Named after the colour of the first ascensionist after cleaning off the pitch. Can be a little dusty.
Gary Gibson, 2000

The next route takes the centre of a prominent pillar formed by two wide cracks.

6 Orange Outang ★ F7b
24m The lower wall below the pillar leads to a ledge. The centre of the pillar above gives fingery and bold wall climbing to finish via the striking thin crack in the headwall. Always clean.
Gary Gibson, 2000

7 Clockwork Orange ★ F7a
18m The right-hand edge of the tower is gained via a faint crack and tricky bulge below. Hard moves to the start the upper arête.
Gary Gibson, 2000

8 Orange Alert ★ F6c
25m A massive pitch. Climb the right edge of the lower block to a ledge in the corner. The face on the right provides a long sustained pitch with the main difficulties 6m above the ledge.
Gary Gibson, 2000

Streaming Walls

These are the blackened walls to the right. Dampness or even a stream, surprise, surprise, more often than not accompanies these. When dry there are some fine pitches here although they will need cleaning before an ascent can be made. All of the routes offer technical and fingery face climbs.

The wall faces in a southerly direction and usually dries out in June, July and August.

Mick Carr on Orange Outang,
F7b (opposite page).
Photo: David Simmonite.

❾ Black and Blue   **F6c**

11m A good little route taking the blue streak 10m right of the corner. Fingery.
Gary Gibson, 2000

❿ Stream On   **F7a**

18m A tricky start and the upper wall via the left-hand side of a prominent overlap. A little hollow in the upper section of the route.
Gary Gibson, 2000

⓫ The Streaming Dream   ★ **F7a+**

20m The fine faint groove in the lower wall and the centre of the wall through an overlap above. A superb route when dry and clean.
Gary Gibson, 2000

⓬ Streamline   ★ **F7b**

22m The centre of the lower wall just to the right and the blunt rib above. Bold and fingery high up. Remains cleanest when dry.
Gary Gibson, Mark Elwell, 2000

⓭ A Drip Round the Ear   **F7a**

12m The left-hand side of the short, sharp arête to the right, with hard, fingery moves. Good when clean.
Gary Gibson, 2000

⓮ A Drip off the Old Block   **F6a+**

12m The obvious right-facing corner gives pleasant enough climbing when clean, which it usually isn't.
Gary Gibson, 2000

Monsterosity Walls

These are the walls to the right of the corner of A Drip off the Old Block. The reasons for the name are obvious - their sheer size. Here will be found two of the longest sport climbs in the Peak if not the whole of Britain. Again, unfortunately, the dust syndrome applies.

These walls face south and gain the sun until 4pm. They dry relatively quickly.

⓯ Cause Célèbre   ★ **F7b**

15m The blunt right arête of the corner line gives a fingery and excellent pitch. Always clean enough to climb.
Gary Gibson, 2000

The next four routes begin from a terrace atop a frozen bank of mud. This can be traversed from left to right or ascended carefully on its right-hand side. A fixed rope may be in place across the wall, which will be appreciated by mountaineers of a nervous disposition.

⓰ Sandstone Story   **F6b+**

18m A direct line up the jug-rimmed wall to the right following a faint rib in places. Good climbing but needs cleaning beforehand.
Gary Gibson, 2000

⓱ Sandsite   **F6b+**

18m The next line to the right via a scoop high up. Sandier than its neighbour and a little care needs to be taken with the rock towards the top.
Gary Gibson, Dave Law, Warren, 2000

⓲ In The End   ★ ★ ★ **F7b**

32m When clean, this is a truly magnificent route. It aims for the impressive flat headwall at the top of the cliff. A hard move on the lower wall and a problematic bulge give access to this. The headwall is sustained leading to an impressive and climactic crux.
Gary Gibson, 2000

⓳ Raven Calling   ★ **F7a**

18m The right-hand arête of the lower wall gives a shorter and more amenable pitch. Low in the grade.
Gary Gibson, Simon Rice, 2000

The next route begins by a prominent pinnacle of rock, a finger pointing towards heaven, and the direction of your ascent.

⓴ Too Monsterosity   ★ ★ **F7a**

45m The longest single pitch sport climb in Britain? A stunning climb with a mountain atmosphere to it. Start 5m to the left of the pinnacle and follow the line of bolts, eighteen in all. Designed for a double lower-off on a 60m rope. Some say a 70m rope gets you back to the ground.
Gary Gibson, 2000

Marble Wall

The wall at the top right-hand corner of the quarry contains two sections; the calcite encrusted wall facing in the direction of the road and the Morsels Wall slanting up the hill to its right. The Marble Wall gains its name from its appearance and offers a number of unusual routes for the Peak due to their rock formation. It is clearly obvious by its 'No Climbing' signs, one spelt incorrectly.

The wall faces south, gets all the sun that is going and makes an ideal spring venue. It takes a little seepage after rain and can be a little dusty. There has even been a seat constructed below the wall!

The routes are described from left to right, beginning with the leaning wall at the end of the face.

㉑ Shattered ★ F6c+
12m The innocuous-looking overhanging wall at the left end of the face provides a fine pitch. Take the upper wall at its centre.
Gary Gibson, 2000

㉒ Unstained F6b
12m A steep wall above a block to the right gains a

chimney. Exit quickly left to a well-positioned arête.
Gary Gibson, Simon Rice, 2000

㉓ Calcite Consequence ★ F6a+
12m A fine warm-up. The short steep arête forming the edge of the main wall is followed by the hanging groove above.
Gary Gibson, 2000

㉔ The Calc Spur ★ ★ F6c
12m A super little pitch. The shallow hanging scoop to the right leads to an excellent climax above the flake on the headwall.
Gary Gibson, Tim Gallagher, 2000

㉕ Brandy Snaps ★ F7a+
12m Climb straight up the smooth-looking wall just right. Technical right to the top with a run-out finale thrown in for good measure. The 'snaps' are inedible and subject to change!
Gary Gibson, 2000

㉖ The Calcspa ★ ★ F6b
12m Fine climbing via the obvious crack in the centre of the wall. Hard starting moves and a technical finish.
Gary Gibson, 2000

㉗ Frozen Moment ★ **F6b+**
12m Fine sustained climbing up the calcite-ridden face to the right. Great holds and fine moves. Needs dry conditions.
Gary Gibson, 2000

㉘ Paneful **F6b**
12m The 'chute' in the centre of the wall leads to a fine upper section.
Gary Gibson, Simon Rice, 2000

㉙ In the Flow **F6c+**
12m The left-hand groove of two, taking the bulge with some fine moves up the black calcite face above.
Gary Gibson, 2000

㉚ Glass Back **F6a+**
12m The right-hand shallow groove is exited by a tricky move to gain a crack and slab above.
Gary Gibson, 2000

㉛ Mirrored ★ **F7a**
12m The centre of the smooth black wall gives a hard start soon easing after the break. Difficult to read.
Gary Gibson, Dave Law, Tim Gallagher, 2000

㉜ Born Slippy ★ **F6c+**
12m Sporty to say the least. A sinuous crack with a thread hold leads to bold climbing on the face above.
Gary Gibson, 2000

㉝ That Shard **F6a**
12m The right-hand route of the wall via a wide crack and scoop. Can be dusty.
Gary & Hazel Gibson, 2000

Morsels Wall

A relatively nondescript wall angling up towards the Marble Wall. The wall faces to the west and gets any afternoon sunshine going. This is a reasonable spot for its 'warm-up' climbs.

㉞ It's a Steal **F5**
12m The conglomerate wall and bulge to the left. Step right to finish.
Gary Gibson, 2000

㉟ It's a Deal **F6a**
12m The line six metres to the right via a blunt rib and leftwards crack in the wall.
Gary Gibson, 2000

㊱ Bobby's Bits **F6b**
12m A hard starting sequence gains a ledge. Finish steeply rightwards.
Gary & Hazel Gibson, 2000

㊲ Succulent Rib ★ **F6c**
12m Just that. The clean white rib in the centre of the wall gives a few hard moves followed by a problematic overlap.
Gary Gibson, 2000

㊳ Tubby Tommy **F6b**
12m A direct route taking the rib and overlap to the same belay.
Gary Gibson, 2000

㊴ Tasty Morsels **F6a**
12m The final route gains a vague leftwards line above an overlap.
Gary Gibson, 2000

Gary Gibson on The Calcspa, F6b
(page 79). Photo: Carl Ryan.

Intake Quarry

O.S. Ref. **SK270550**   Altitude: **320m a.s.l.**

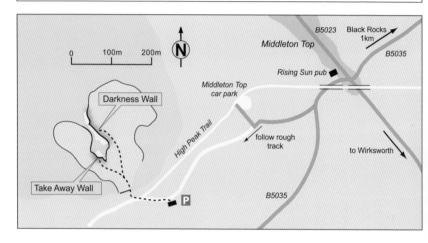

Over the years this quarry has had a number of worthwhile traditional style routes added to the huge vertical walls in the back of the quarry. However, recently, a number of long, quality sport pitches have been added on what can only be called unusual and 'fused rock'. Generally speaking the main routes on the Darkness Wall are very long by Peak District standards (20m+) and although they may be in need of a little traffic, will prove well worth visiting. The Take Away Wall, a smaller, sunnier wall, also offers a number of other good pitches.

The climbing

Twenty five routes, almost all single pitch, up to 25m in height. Most of these are in the F6 range, with a couple of harder offerings. The Take Away Wall offers steep to slightly overhanging climbs on fairly good, rough rock with positive crimpy holds. On the Darkness Wall, routes have a more intimidating feel. They have good variety, including face, crack and arête climbs. At the time of writing some of these climbs are dusty, but there is no doubt that with more regular traffic, these will become fine routes.

Conditions & aspect

This is a very fresh, open quarry, as it lies more or less at the top of a hill. The smaller Take Away Wall gets lots of light and is quick drying, while the larger Darkness Wall, as would be expected, gets little sun. All quick drying.

Parking & approach

Approach from Middleton Top, turning uphill at the Rising Sun pub, and take the first right after a bridge, signposted Middleton Top and High Peak Trail. This tarmac road takes a sharp right: continue

Take Away Wall

straight down the gravel track to a parking place by the second building on the left. The quarry gates lie straight ahead, covered in the usual unwelcoming signs. **Walk-in:** 5 to 10 minutes.

Traditional climbs

The major walls at the back and sides of the quarry contain about 25 traditional routes, mostly in the E1 to E3 range, with one E6. These are mostly long, intimidating crack-lines, although there are a few ENP protected routes. They were developed by Bill Birch, Nick Taylor and Rowland Edwards between 1999 and 2000. See introduction for further details.

Take Away Wall

A small, compact and somewhat insignificant-looking wall with quite good rock and some worthwhile pitches. Situated on the fringes of the quarry, this face is best located by taking a direct route to the outer 'peninsula' walls of the quarry towards it left-hand bowl. It is the only worthwhile piece of rock outside of the main horseshoe of the quarry.

The wall faces south-west, and gets all the sunshine going from 11am in the morning and provides an

ideal evening venue. It gets very little seepage.

1 Crispy Duck   F6b
12m Exit a small alcove with blind moves onto a steep face.
Gary & Phil Gibson, 2003

2 Prawn Crackers   ★ F6c
12m The right-hand line leads to the same belay and provides a better and more testing route. Fingery and surprisingly sustained.
Gary & Phil Gibson, 2003

3 The Big Take Out   ★ F6a
11m The obvious thin crack-line gives a good steep pitch.
Gary, Hazel & Phil Gibson, 2003

4 Who Flung Dung   F6b+
11m A tricky start left of the bolts leads to much easier climbing above.
Gary & Phil Gibson, 2003

5 Blue Moon Night   F6c+
11m Very technical moves to start. Easy above the second bolt runner.
Gary & Phil Gibson, 2003

Darkness Wall

6 Chop Suicide ★ F6b
15m Fine climbing on the steep juggy wall to the right. The belay lies at the back of the ledge.
Gary, Hazel & Phil Gibson, 2003

7 Les Chinoises F6a
15m The next steep line, a vague rib, to a steep finale. Again the belay lies well back.
Gary Gibson, 2003

8 Order Number 69 F6a+
11m An obvious pod-shaped crack above a ledge. Worthwhile.
Gary Gibson, 2003

9 The Golden Duck F6a
11m The final and most right-hand line on the wall.
Gary Gibson, 2003

Darkness Wall

An impressive section of cliff, this large dark wall faces back towards the main quarry and gets little sunshine. Its height and unusually 'fused' nature gives a series of routes untypical of the Peak, especially when you are the only climbers in the quarry. The routes may be slightly dusty but after further climbers have passed this way the routes will become a lot cleaner and undoubtedly very popular.

The wall faces north-east, only getting sun in the early morning. Not much seepage but damp in winter.

The routes are described from left to right beginning with a high level wall above a grassy platform. All the routes have double bolt belays at their base.

10 Join the Dots F5
12m The left-hand route gives the easiest line in the quarry and is a pleasant addition.
Gary & Hazel Gibson, 2003

11 See Spot Run ★ F6b+
12m The central line, taking a slight pillar, gives a fine route with a hint of atmosphere and exposure.
Gary, Hazel & Phil Gibson, 2003

12 In a Dash F6c
12m The right-hand pillar is worthwhile but not as fine as its neighbours.
Gary Gibson, 2003

The next series of routes begins at a lower level, at the left-hand side of the wall proper.

13 The Clumps ★ F5
25m The left-hand side of the first wall gives an exercise in 'lump' climbing. There is more than one lump or two. "May be in need of a '*jet-wash*'".
Gary, Hazel & Phil Gibson, 2003

14 A Sharp Intake of Breath ★★ F6b
25m The centre of the first wall provides a classic pitch with a definite crux at 10m. Superb sustained climbing above and below.
Gary, Hazel & Phil Gibson, 2003

⓯ Brain Candy　　　　　　**F6b**

20m The right-hand side of the wall, whilst not quite so fine, gives a number of excellent moves high up.
Gary Gibson, 2003

⓰ Stinking Rose　　　　★ **F6c**

20m The next line begins via a prominent overlap in a corner. A fingery start reaches the main break. The moves above provide the crux and give access to a very pleasant finish.
Gary Gibson, 2003

⓱ Rabbit Proof Fence　　★ **F6c+**

25m An excellent sustained pitch situated 8m to the right. The occasional hollow hold and thin flake is compensated for by a superb sustained upper wall.
Gary & Phil Gibson, 2003

The next route is situated on the impressive black wall next to a semi-detached pinnacle at half height.

⓲ Intolerable Cruelty　　★★ **F7a**

25m Superb climbing following the arête of a large block and a superb and intricate upper wall. A half-height ledge provides some respite.
GaryGibson, 2003

⓳ Tucker's Grave　　　★★ **F6c+**

25m A fine outing taking the centre of the black wall. A straightforward start culminates in a technical and fingery sequence of moves to gain the belay.
Gary, Hazel & Phil Gibson, 2003

⓴ Plum Tuckered Out　　★★ **F6b**

25m The right-hand twin gives a fine pitch of its grade finishing via the crack in the headwall and a short though deceptively fingery finale.
Gary, Hazel & Phil Gibson, 2003

㉑ Friar Tuck　　　　　　**F6c**

22m A short tricky wall above the ledge leads to a thin crack-line in the wall above.
Gary Gibson, 2003

㉒ That'll Teach 'em　　★★ **F7a+**

18m The lower wall leads to a difficult sequence to reach the black wall proper. Difficult fingery moves follow in quick succession before the belay is gained

above an overlap.
Gary Gibson, 2003

㉓ A Jam's as Good as a Rest ★★ **E3 5c**

18m Climb the obvious crack, moving right to follow it through the overlap, where the difficulties are just beginning. Superb, sustained climbing.
Nick Taylor, 2003

㉔ Dead Ringer　　　　★★ **F6c+**

18m The fine sheer side-wall to the right offers a gleaming white face and a classic wall climb on bubbly porous rock. Superb steep climbing.
Gary Gibson, 2003

The next route takes an impressive line up a huge square-cut chimney to the right.

㉕ Our Kid's Orchid　　★★ **F6c, F7a**

30m The lower wall, left of the crack, gives an intricate few moves past an overlap. Move right to the belay. The arête above now provides a classic exercise in lay backing and face climbing.
Gary & Hazel Gibson, 2003

The huge walls extending right from the Darkness Wall, and right across the back of the quarry, contain a good number of challenging, high-quality traditional climbs.The last sport climb is on the orange buttress opposite the jutting prow (containing Take Away wall). This buttress, again, contains a good number of traditional climbs. In its centre is a slabby arête.

㉖ Trunkline　　　　　　**F7a+**

14m Start up the shallow corner then climb the slabby arête on its right side.
Gary Gibson, 2002

The Buxton Area 3

Gary Gibson on When
Reason Sleeps, F7a+, (page 177).
Photo: David Simmonite.

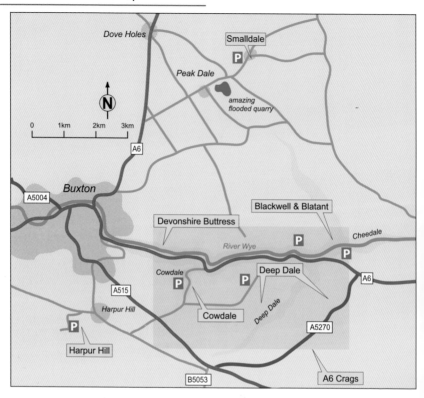

Below: the A6 Area crags

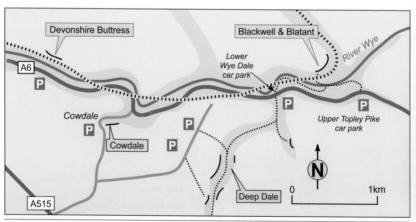

Devonshire Buttress

O.S. Ref. **SK080726**   Altitude: **300m a.s.l.**

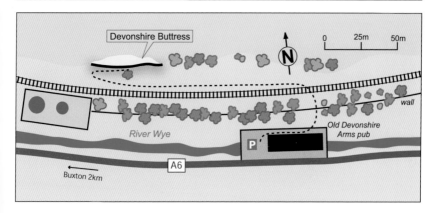

(Also known as Beer House Buttress)
This is a very pleasant little crag with an open aspect and good, quickly drying nature. It is the small cliff, very easily identifiable as the white, gleaming wall above the water treatment plant 2km out of Buxton on the A6 when heading towards Bakewell.

It is a good venue for a quick visit, as it is easily visible from the road to check conditions, and the walk-in is very short. There are not a lot of routes, but it will easily reward one or two evening visits.

The climbing

Eighteen routes in the F6s and low F7s on steep natural limestone. The nature of the climbing lends itself to short technical test-pieces on small face holds not unlike Rubicon Wall in Water-cum-Jolly, but without the attendant competitive nature.

Conditions & aspect

The cliff faces south and gets any sunshine going from late in the morning. After long spells of wet weather the cliff can, however, take some degree of seepage, although this is not too bad, and due to its exposed and sunny aspect, can easily be dry at the end of the winter. The rock is clean and sound.

Parking & approach

This is relatively straightforward. Take the A6 out of Buxton heading towards Bakewell. The first building on the left-hand side of the road (1.5 km from Safeway) is the remnants of the Devonshire Arms where suitable parking can be had, but unfortunately no longer any beer. The same spot can be identified when coming in the other direction, as it is just after the last of 4 overhead railroad bridges. From the parking, hop over the wall behind the pub and carefully follow the **LIVE** railway leftwards to below the crag. Gain this by scrambling up the banking on the left. **Walk-in:** 5 easy minutes.

The routes are described beginning with a short route to the left of some obvious capping overhangs.

 Nice Melons   **F6b**
11m A poor route up a rib and short bulge at the left-hand side of the crag.
Gary Gibson, 1997

 Gimme Shelter   **F7a**
11m This climbs through the capping roofs at the left end of the crag by two hard moves. Worthwhile.
Nadim Siddiqui, Colin Struthers, David Simmonite, 1997

❸ And the Roof Fell In   F7b
11m Well-named. It is based round a short and very hard section over the right-hand side of the capping overhang.
Gary Gibson, 1997

❹ Infantada   ★ F6b+
11m Another blunt rib to and through a bulge. Intricate climbing.
Colin Struthers, Nadim Siddiqui, David Simmonite, 1997

❺ Last Man First   ★ F7a
12m A technical start leads to an excellent upper section above the prominent alcove.
Gary Gibson, 1997

❻ Chain Reaction   F6c+
12m A blunt rib leads to a series of fine moves rightwards through the small overlap. Probably best gained from the next route.
Nadim Siddiqui, 1997

❼ Jewfish   ★ F7b
12m The desperately thin and crimpy direct start to Chain Reaction. Gold bolt runners.
Gary Gibson, 1997

❽ Jihad   ★ F7b
12m Marginally easier than Jewfish but still hard to flash. A direct and fingery line from just to the left of the tree.
Nadim Siddiqui, 1997

❾ Here   ★ F7a
12m Thin fingery face climbing from just right of the tree. Blind moves on hidden holds- typical of the crag!
Gary Gibson, 1997

❿ We are not Alone   F6c
12m The last route before the step up. Good climbing with a long stretch left at the crux.
Nadim Siddiqui, 1997

The next routes begin from the terrace.

⓫ Little Brown Men   F6c
12m From the left-hand end of the terrace, climb the thin and technical wall.
Nadim Siddiqui, 1997

⓬ Clotted Cream   ★ F6a
12m A fine warm-up straight up the centre of the white wall above the step up in the path. A little gem.
Gary Gibson, 1979, solo

Nadim 'Sid' Siddiqui on Clotted
Cream. F6a (opposite page).
Photo: David Simmonite.

⑬ **The Age of Reason** ★ **F6b**
12m A shallow white groove to the right of the white wall finishing via a compact face.
Nadim Siddiqui, 1997

⑭ **Savage Girth** ★ **F6b+**
12m Fingery from the word go. Another shallow groove and faint rib.
David Simmonite, Nadim Siddiqui, 1997

⑮ **Idiot Nation** **F6c**
12m A series of very bouldery moves lead to a shallow crack on the left-hand side of an open groove.
Nadim Siddiqui, 1997

⑯ **It's Uranus** **F7a**
9m Two desperate moves up and over a bulge.
Gary Gibson, 1997

⑰ **Mercury Dripping** **F6c+**
9m More bouldery action to the left of a scoop.
Gary Gibson, 1997

⑱ **Men are from Mars, Women are from Venus** **F6c**
9m A route through the scoop. Again, bouldery.
Nadim Siddiqui, 1997

Kim Leyland on Windows 95, F6a+
(page 98). Photo: David Parry.

Blackwell & Blatant

O.S. Ref. **SKIII728**   Altitude: **255m a.s.l.**

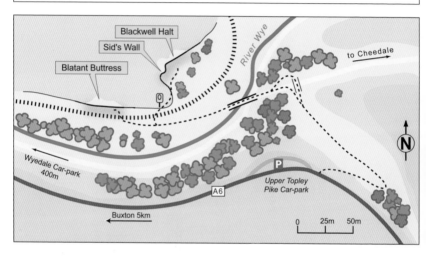

These are two good crags lying near the railway line at the head of Chee Dale. They both offer a good collection of F6 routes, and are only minutes apart. Blackwell Halt is one of the more popular venues in this guide, with good, long mid-grade sport climbing on solid rock, set peacefully in a pretty meadow giving splendid views down past Plum Buttress to Chee Dale. Blatant Buttress lies only two minutes away giving more varied climbing, with the added attraction of quarry trains rumbling underneath every now and then.

The climbing

About 30 routes, almost all in the F6s and well-bolted. Blatant Buttress is a steep wall of grey limestone, where the better routes are generally in the higher grades. With its grooves, ramps and walls, it manages to give a good variety of styles, despite being quite small. The main wall of Blackwell Halt is deceptively steep and provides a welcome number of high-quality middle-grade sport climbs of a similar style: technical and fingery with the occasional good resting place.

Conditions & aspect

Both are fairly quick-drying venues with good sunshine, and a good bet for the early spring months and even in winter during a good dry spell. **Blatant Buttress:** The buttress dries very quickly and faces into the sun for most of the day. In the winter and early spring months the sun dips below the skyline relatively early and makes the crags a cold venue. The walls take little seepage except after long deluges of rain. It can be plagued by midges in humid weather. **Blackwell Halt:** The walls dry relatively quickly in the spring months and stay dry in light rain. They get the rays of the sun from early morning until about 3pm but can become midgy on a summer's evening or in humid weather.

Parking & approach

Note: The approach to these crags demands the crossing of railway lines that are still frequently used. It is important to pay the utmost care when crossing these.

The Traditional Approach: Park in the Topley Pike

Rhys the Snowboarder on Gopherspace, F6b (page 98). Photo: Niall Grimes.

car-park at the top of the hill, 5km to the south of Buxton on the A6. Descend the steep hillside by going through a gate at the upper end of the car-park, then following a good path towards some trees near the head of the little valley. From here, cut back left and walk downhill. Please do not take any short-cuts, as the hillside is protected for conservation reasons. From the old railway track at the bottom (now a public footpath), walk leftwards through an old gate, crossing a bridge over the River Wye, then through some trees to reach a 'live' railway track. Blatant Buttress is on the side of the track, 50m to the left; for Blackwell Halt, cross the track immediately and with care, and scramble up a banking behind a yellow sign to reach the quarry. **Walk-in:** the approach takes just over 10 minutes, although it's just over 15 to get back out again, so save some energy for that hill.

Alternatively, for **The Gentle Approach,** park further down the hill at the Wyedale car-park (pay & display, or park just outside the quarry across the road), and follow the Monsal Trail along the tranquil river for a few hundred metres until it climbs up by the third railroad bridge. This is the bridge mentioned for the above approach. **Walk-in:** 10 minutes.

Blatant Buttress

The cliff is divided into two distinct buttresses by an obvious slabby area. The right-hand buttress is clearly marked by the graffiti 'KILL FLETCHER'.

The wall faces in a southerly direction and gets sun in the late morning and afternoon.

1 For the Good of the Cause   **F5+**

18m   Climb a faint rib and ledgy corner.
Brian Cropper, Nadim Siddiqui, (both led) 1998

2 Close to the Edge   **F6b**

18m   Climb the wall left of a corner and finish up the wall above, as directly and as closely as possible to the arête.
Nadim Siddiqui, Brian Cropper, (both led) 1998

3 Every Breath you Take   ★ **F6b+**

18m   Spaced bolt runners but not run out! Move left from the corner and climb the wall right of the arête via a crack-line and large ledge (tricky clip). The best route on this buttress.
Nadim Siddiqui, Brian Cropper, (both led) 1998

Blatant Buttress

4 **Eye Catching Cod Piece** ★ **F6b+**
18m Continues direct up the wall above the start of
Every Breath You Take, with a crux section crossing
a roof above the black patch.
Nadim Siddiqui, Brian Cropper, (both led) 1998

5 **Pipistrelle** **F6a**
18m The rib and groove finishing up the wall above
the ledge.
Brian Cropper, Nadim Siddiqui, (both led) 1998

6 **Rave On** **F6a**
18m The rib to the right.
Brian Cropper, Nadim Siddiqui, (both led) 1998

7 **Chill Out** **F6a+**
18m Average climbing saved by some good final
moves. Ledgy ground 3m right of Rave On leads to
a pleasant slabby finish.
Nadim Siddiqui, Brian Cropper, (both led) 1998

8 **Feel the Beat** ★ **F6b**
18m Tricky moves to enter a vague groove. A zig-zag

line on the slab gives another good finish.
Nadim Siddiqui, Brian Cropper, (both led) 1998

9 **Emission Control** ★ **F7a+**
18m The wall left of the graffiti is steep and fingery.
The finish, via the groove, is technical and superb.
Nadim Siddiqui, Jim Burton, 1998

10 **Good Vibrations** ★ **F7a+**
18m This is the wall through the right-hand side of
the graffiti, bearing left to join the last route. More
good climbing.
Nadim Siddiqui, Brian Cropper, Colin Struthers, 1998

11 **Loco-Motion** ★ **F7a**
18m The wall just left of the ramp leads to a hard
finishing wall on hidden holds.
Nadim Siddiqui, Brian Cropper, 1998

12 **Love is a Swallow** **F6a+**
18m The wall above the ramp-line. Steep at the
finale.
S Barker, Nadim & Rehan Siddiqui, Brian Cropper, 1998

Blackwell Halt

Walk down the track for 50m to a yellow sign, then scramble up the bank. The next walls are on the quarried section just in front.

Sid's Wall

An aperitif for the main wall, this subsidiary wall stands 30m to its front. It consists of a fine juggy headwall with a lower smoother section which provides the main difficulties.

The wall faces south-east, and gets the sun until about 3pm.

① Ernie   **F6c**
12m Difficult and fingery moves lead to the break. Juggy and easier above.
Andy Theaker, Nadim Siddiqui, Colin Struthers, 1995

② Defrag   **F6c**
12m Similar in character but marginally easier. Again a hard start leads to an easier finish.
Nadim Siddiqui, Colin Struthers, 1995

③ Anoraks and Trainspotters   **F6b**
12m Hard moves lead up the obvious flake to gain the juggy headwall.
Nadim & Rehan Siddiqui, 1995

Sid's Wall

④ Micro-nerd   **F6b+**
12m The short, rippled lower wall, crux, is followed by the left-hand side of arête above.
Nadim & Rehan Siddiqui, 1995

Main Wall

This is the larger wall to the right, bounded on its left-hand side by a shallow groove topped by a platform at 6m. All of the routes on this wall have a similar feel to them but offer, in the most part, excellent climbing for those operating in the lower end of the sport climbing grades. The first routes start from the platform and are then described from left to right across the wall.

The wall faces south-east, getting the sun till about 3pm.

⑤ Micro Chip   ★ **F6c+**
9m The compact and smooth-looking wall above the terrace. Short and intense.
Bill Birch, Rick Gibbon, 1995

⑥ Modem   **F6a+**
9m The easier wall to the right leads directly to the tree. A good warm-up.
Bill Birch, Rick Gibbon, 1995

The Main Wall

Returning back to the lower level is:

7 **CD Romp**   **E2 5c**
15m A traditional route climbing the corner to finish via the thin crack above the ledge.
Rick Gibbon, Bill Birch, 1995

8 **Arapaho Connection**   ★ ★ **F6b+**
15m The best route on the crag. Starting just right of the corner, the wall and overlap above give fine sustained climbing.
Bill Birch, Rick Gibbon, 1995

9 **Hard Drive**   ★ **F6c**
15m A tricky start leads to the centre of the wall above, which gives further hard climbing.
Rick Gibbon, Bill Birch, 1995

10 **Mega Byte**   ★ **F6b**
15m After an awkward move to gain a ledge, take a direct line up face. Eases above the break.
Bill Birch, Rick Gibbon, 1995

11 **Gopherspace**   **F6b**
15m More of the same to the right, this time taking a small roof on its left-hand side.
Bill Birch, Rick Gibbon, 1995

12 **Windows 95**   ★ **F6a+**
15m The roof, taken centrally, gives access to the delightful wall above.
Rick Gibbon, Bill Birch, 1995

13 **Falling Icons**   **F6b**
15m The right-hand side of the overlap. A tricky

move / long reach on the upper wall lies in wait.
Rick Gibbon, Bill Birch, 1995

⑭ She got the Bosch, I got the Drill
                            ★ **F6b**

12m From a short way up the slope on the right, climb the wall to a ledge and finish directly above. Reachy.
Bill Birch, Rick Gibbon, 1995

⑮ Waste Bin   **F6a+**
12m Starting slightly higher up the slope, climb the right-hand side of the vague groove to a roof.
Bill Birch, Rick Gibbon, 1995

The final two routes begin from the top of the slope.

⑯ The Hacker   **F6b+**
12m Left-hand of two routes, with two hard moves.
Bill Birch, Rick Gibbon, 1995

⑰ E Mail   **F6b**
12m The right-hand line. Fingery.
Bill Birch, Rick Gibbon, 1995

⑱ Surfing the Net   **F6c**
25m An interesting midway girdle can be had by traversing the wall from left to right. Climb to the second bolt on Modem then traverse right at more or less mid-height, clipping 11 bolts *en route*, to lower off E Mail. A medium nut is useful for the section leaving CD Romp.
Rick Gibbon, 1996

Cowdale (a.k.a. Craig-y-Biceps)

O.S. Ref. **SK084722**	Altitude: **315m a.s.l.**

Much has been written about this superb little cliff, most of it derogatory, by those who have not climbed here. On first acquaintance it may appear a small nondescript crag but on direct acquaintance this feels a significant distance from the truth. Steep overhangs, bulges and leaning walls provide a number of intense little problems with big arms a major advantage. Indeed, it has been christened Craig-y-Biceps.

Conditions & aspect
The cliff takes seepage in wintertime and after prolonged periods of rain and can sometimes be cloaked in chick-weed. This in itself is easily removed when dry. Best visited after a good dry spell later in the season. The setting is beautiful, and unique among Peak limestone crags. Beware the thick nettle growth on the approach to the crag, and perhaps reconsider those short trousers. It is north-facing, and gets virtually no sun.

The climbing
Generally harder routes. Steep and powerful on natural limestone.

Parking & approach
A little road leads off the A6 on the apex of a sharp horseshoe bend (marked 'Unsuitable for caravans'). Take this road, and follow it up to parking at Cowdale village. Walk back down to the crag. Parking below the cliff may well cause an obstruction on a very narrow road so please park sensibly. **Walk-in:** One downhill minute although committed sport climbers may wish to observe that the downhill walk becomes an uphill one on the way back.

1 **J.L.N.O.E.** ★ **F7b+**
12m A short intense sequence through the bulge right of the prominent crack.
Gary Gibson, 1991

2 **Much Monkey Magic** ★ ★ **F7a**
12m The overhanging crack to the right feels very tough for its grade although it is well worth the effort. Superbly named.
Gary Gibson, 1983

3 **Otto di Catania** ★ **F7a+**
12m The imposing bulge to the right of the crack. Gaining it is tricky, and passing it may require a flying leap or just brute force.
Gary Gibson, 1991

4 **Dazed and Amazed** ★ **F7b+**
12m Stiff moves over a tricky bulge gain the break. Step right and make hard moves through the main bulge to reach a shallow groove above.
Gary Gibson, 1991

5 **The Philandering Sons of Magic Women** **F7a**
11m The twisting crack-line is gained by powerful moves and followed strenuously.
Gary Gibson, 1991

6 **A Wild Man from Way Back When** ★ **F7a+**
11m A super, power-packed pitch direct through the bulge and overlap.
Gary Gibson, 1991

7 **Duelling Biceps** **F7a**
11m A short, powerful pitch via the box-shaped recess.
Graham Parkes, 1989

8 **A Woman in Wellingtons** **F7b**
11m The powerful bulge to the right via a reconstructed hole. High in the grade.
Gary Gibson, 1999

9 **Wet yer Whistle** ★ **F7b+**
12m The powerful bulge to the right complete with a very painful glued on hold. Despite this, it provides a good problem, and one that is high in its grade.
Gary Gibson, 1995

⑩ The Main Motor Mile ★ ★ F7a+

12m The original route, and still the classic of the crag. The overhanging finger-crack yields to brute force and ingenuity. You may have one of these, but what's the chances of having both?
Gary Gibson, 1983

⑪ Pingham's Roof ★ ★ F7c+

12m The square-cut roof to the right is taken at its centre. Fingery moves gain it and a gymnastic sequence leads through it.
Paul Ingham, 1995

⑫ Laughing at the Rain ★ ★ ★ F7c

12m One of the best short hard routes in the Peak District. The overhanging prow is gained by a powerful sequence and provides a jug-fest above.
Gary Gibson, 1995

⑬ Mesmerised ★ ★ F7b

12m The large hanging corner at the right-hand side of the cliff gained by a series of gymnastic moves leftwards through the roof below.
Gary Gibson, 1987

⑭ You Know U.F.O.s ★ F7a+

11m Go up directly from start of Mesmerised by one further hard move.
Gary Gibson, 1991

⑮ Euphoric F7a

11m More gymnastics to the right lead to a short-lived wall.
Gary Gibson, 1995

COWDALE
Please drive
carefully

Deep Dale

O.S. Ref. **SK098715**   Altitude: **315m a.s.l.**

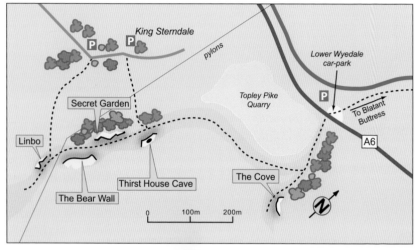

Another rarely frequented dale with a mixture of traditional and sport climbing alike. The crags face in a variety of directions, so you can have a good choice between sunshine and shade. It is best enjoyed by visiting a few of the venues in one visit.

The climbing

Almost 30 bolted routes, single pitch, with a good spread from very low up to some tricky F7s. Each crag has its own individual character, although most tend to provide fingery wall climbs on vertical rock.

Traditional climbs

Deep Dale has a history of traditional and aid climbing stretching back to the 1960s. In the 1970s, climbers such as Phil Burke, Graham Warren, Bob Conway, Chris Jackson and Tom Proctor continued the development here. Many additions took place in the 1980s from Simon Nadin, Richard Davies and Paul Mitchell, amongst others, and in latter years, Nick Taylor has been keeping the tradition alive. The area is also home to almost 100 such routes, varying in quality from the terrible up to superb crack-lines. Many are worth checking out. See main introduction for details.

Conditions & aspect

Some crags face east, getting morning sun (Secret Garden and Linbo), others face west and get afternoon and evening sun (Bear Wall, Thirst House and the Cove). Some crags seep a little in winter, and the Secret Garden, due to its steep nature and tree cover, can stay dry in light rain.

Approaches

There are two main approaches into the dale, the first most applicable for the Cove and the second for the remainder of the cliffs.

Approach One: Park at the lower Topley Pike car park 4km east of Buxton on the A6 and follow the track alongside the quarry entrance past two small ponds and into the dale. The Cove lies 300m ahead. For the rest of the dale, climb a short steep grassy

bank on the right-hand side of the track and continue up the dale to the rest of the cliffs.

Approach Two: Take the small road to Cowdale from the A6 and go through the small village. Take the first turning left after the village and follow this road to the small church at King Sterndale: park

here. Follow the public footpath behind the cottage opposite to the church across two fields and descend into the dale. The Thirst House Cave lies at the foot of the slope, slightly up the dale.

This dale has been acquired

in recent times by the Derbyshire Wildlife Trust because of its outstanding natural value. It is a protected prime site of international importance. The Trust would prefer if there was no climbing here at all, but is initially prepared to accept very low levels of activity on established routes. It is absolutely vital that if this concession is to be maintained there is no damage to vegetation - this includes grasses, ferns, mosses and lichens besides more showy flowering plants. Scree slopes are particularly vulnerable to disturbance and must always be left undisturbed as they host a special and fragile flora.

The Southern Side

The crags are described starting on the southern side and working their way up the dale. The first of these is closer to the A6 than it is to the other crags.

The Cove

This pleasant little cliff is situated approximately 300m from the main A6 and is reached in a brisk 5 minutes walk. It faces south-west and gets any sunshine that is going, dries quickly and offers a handful of worthwhile routes.

The Cove

❶ **Bob Slopes**   **F6c+**
12m Bouldery moves on horrible holds gives access to an easy 7m of slab!
Gary Gibson, 1995

❷ **The Beast**   ★ **F7b+**
12m Another very bouldery sequence on perfect pocketed rock to the right. Short and mean.
Gary Gibson, 1995

❸ **The English Inpatient**   ★ **F7b**
12m Tricky undercut moves to the left of the prominent crack lead to a stiff pull on crimps to reach the easier face above.
Gary Gibson, 1997

❹ **Old Nick**   ★ **E1 5b**
12m The thin crack-line. A better alternative, **Nicodemus**, E1 5c, crosses the slab above diagonally leftwards (Nick Taylor, 1999).
Bob Conway, 1979

❺ **Instrumentally Yours**   **F7a**
12m The centre of the white pillar direct to twin trees. A tad fragile but worthwhile.
Gary Gibson, 1995

❻ **The Edge of Donnybrooks**   **F7a**
12m The right-hand arête of the wall. A difficult overlap but contrived above.
Gary Gibson, 1995

The Upper Dale - Thirst House Cave

The rest of the cliffs are best reached by the second approach described in the introduction. Once you have descended into the dale, turn right to find the cave. It provides some very powerful test-pieces on good quality rock. Once dry in the springtime, the cliff stays dry for the majority of the summer and is climbable quickly after rain.

The wall faces in a north-westerly direction and only receives sunshine in the late afternoon / early evening. **Walk-in:** 10-15 minutes.

Thirst House Cave

7 Too Mellow to Bellow   **E5 6b**
11m The shallow groove left of the cave is followed past an old peg.
Paul Mitchell, 1985

8 Thirsty Work   ★ **F7b**
11m Steep fingery climbing on the left-hand edge of the cave.
Gary Gibson, 1995

9 Pow Wow   **F7c+**
11m A steep line with a powerful move.
Tom Briggs, 2003

10 Unquenched   **F7c**
11m A desperate sequence through the right-hand side of the roof. Totally bouldery!
Gary Gibson, 1998

The Bear Wall

These walls lie on the same side as the Thirst House Cave and opposite the Secret Garden, slightly further along. Black in appearance and with a number of faint crack-lines, they offer another handful of technical pitches. Gain the cliff by scrambling up to its right-hand side above a lower tier.

The wall faces in a north-westerly direction and gets the sun in the late afternoon / early evening.

The routes are described from left to right, starting with two isolated pitches at the far end of the cliff.

11 Get it Wired   **F7a+**
9m A thin crack-system in complete isolation and so in isolation ye shall struggle. Hideous!
Nadim Siddiqui, 1997

12 Larium   ★ **F7a**
10m Another isolated route with great moves for its length on a blunt overhung arête.
Gary Gibson, Nadim Siddiqui, 1997

The rest of the routes lie on the wall proper.

13 The Bear Necessities   ★ **F7a**
12m The left-hand line of the wall gives a technical bulge and short wall with complicated moves. Low in the grade.
Gary Gibson, Nadim Siddiqui, Colin Struthers, 1997

14 Bear Faced Cheek   ★ **F7a+**
12m Another blind bulge on thin, unhelpful holds. Easier for the tall, just!
Gary Gibson, Nadim Siddiqui, Colin Struthers, 1997

⑮ Bear it All ★ **F7a+**

12m Guess what, another technical bulge, this time harder still.
Gary Gibson, 1997

⑯ Bearly ★ **F5+**

12m Respite. The short wall and excellent thin crack.
Gary Gibson, Neville Barker, 1997

⑰ Bearing All **F6b**

12m A short technical wall leads to a prominent flake.
Gary Gibson, Nadim Siddiqui, 1997

⑱ The Water Method Man **E3 5c**

12m Climb the lower face passing a bolt runner and swing left into a steep thin crack.
Darren Hawkins, 1988

⑲ Setting Free the Bears **E4 6a**

12m Swing right from the start of The Water Method Man and climb the wall above. Avoid the blank central section to the right.
Darren Hawkins, 1988

⑳ Palestine **F6c**

12m Climb a tricky wall then traverse right under the bulge and finish direct up the front of the pillar. A mediocre eliminate. Going directly up from the start of the traverse is **Emmaline** (E1 5c, Bob Conway, 1979).
Nadim Siddiqui, 1997

The Northern Side - Linbo Wall

This is a tiny wall sat opposite the Bear Wall, low in the dale.

㉑ Linbo **F6a+**

8m The short face climb on the left.
Keith Ashton, Seal, 1997

㉒ Shades of Distinction **F6a**

8m The short line to the right leads to the same lower-off.
Seal, Keith Ashton, 1997

Linbo Wall 21 22

The Secret Garden

Continuing down the dale is a clean white wall, almost opposite the Bear Wall, perched above a nondescript lower tier. This is home to a number of traditional routes, all in the HVS-E3 range (the most obvious ones are mentioned here), and a handful of sport pitches. The cliff takes very little seepage and is climbable even in the winter months. It is also worth noting that with its steep nature and overhanging trees, the routes can stay dry in showers.

The walls face in a south-easterly direction and receive any sunshine up until midday.

Gain the face by scrambling easily up to its left-hand side from where its routes are described.

㉓ Costa del Soul **F6c+**

11m A short difficult bulge on the innocuous left-hand face.
Gary Gibson, 1997

㉔ Mosquito Coast **F6c+**

11m The right-hand of the two lines with a few difficult moves. Currently has no bolt runners.
Gary Gibson, 1997

㉕ Ben's Groove ★ **VS 4c**

11m The deep V-groove to the right. The crack exiting this on the left is **Bill's Crack** (HVS 5a, Phil Burke, 1977).
Bob Conway, 1979

26 Half-Way Crack ★ E2 5c
12m Gain and climb the crack.
Phil Burke, 1977

27 The Birdcage ★ F7a+
12m A heavily 'constructed' line on the gleaming white wall in the centre of crag. Good moves on the glued on lumps.
Gary Gibson, 1997

28 Valley of the Birds ★ ★ F7b
12m A super little pitch, the right-hand of the pair. Fingery, with blind moves and gradually increasing difficulties.
Gary Gibson, 1997

29 Tom's Off Day Route ★ E2 5c
12m Climb to the right-hand crack. Traverse left to gain and climb the very sustained groove.
Tom Proctor, 1979

30 Quiet, Shhh, Hush F7a
11m A short and sharp route up the obvious white wall. Again, stuck back together.
Gary Gibson, 1997

31 Midge Dance ★ ★ E3 5c
15m The wall between the two sport routes.
Tom Proctor, 1979

32 Secret Agenda ★ F6c
15m A little gem of a pitch and low in the grade. Flakes and edges lead to a prominent flake and huge tree atop the pitch.
Gary Gibson, 1997

33 Pillar Torque F6b
15m This last route lies at the end of the terrace up the obvious feature. Pleasant enough.
Gary Gibson, 1997

Crag X

O.S. Ref. **SK166708**   Altitude: **150m a.s.l.**

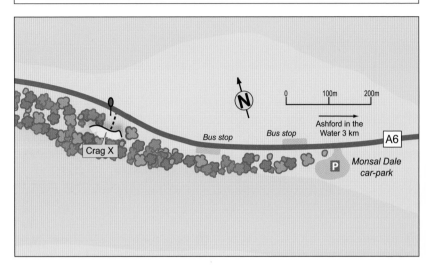

A super little crag with easy access and a pleasant easterly aspect. The intricate character of the rock together with its compact nature make this a very worthwhile venue for an evening visit or in conjunction with another crag on the same day. It is best suited to those operating in the higher grades.

The climbing

Fifteen routes, mainly in the upper F6 and F7 ranges, up to 15m in height. The routes are on slightly overhanging walls, with some roofs thrown in for good measure, and tend to be fierce and fingery. Mostly good quality, natural limestone, and well-bolted.

Conditions & aspect

The crag sits just up from the A6, nestled in thick trees. The setting is pleasant, but not peaceful, although thick summer trees do help to keep the noise of the road down. It only gets sunshine until 11am in the summer, so it is best visited as an escape from the heat, making it less than ideal as a winter venue. Due to the overhanging nature and capping roof, the climbs can stay dry in light rain.

Parking & approach

Locate the Monsal Dale pay & display car-park on the A6 between Buxton and Bakewell. This is on the right, at the bottom of a long hill 5km from the B6049 Blackwell Dale turning when coming from Buxton, or on the left 3km from A6020 Ashford in the Water junction when coming from Bakewell. Park here. Walk towards Buxton, passing a bus stop at 200m, then at 400m, locate a red clearway sign (the 'X' of 'Crag X') on the left-hand side of the road. Strike straight up the hillside to reach the crag after 30m. Thrill seekers, the anti-walking lobby, and those unwilling to pay for parking, may wish to park just below the crag, on the Bakewell side of the sign (parking on the other side can result in a ticket).

At the left-hand side of the cliff is a huge cave, an ideal

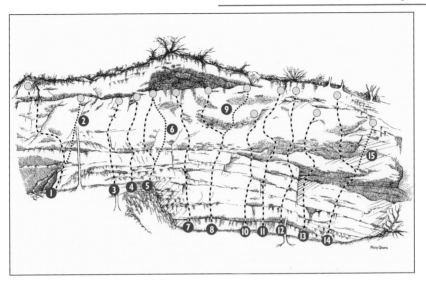

spot to retreat to in a downpour. The first routes lie on the right-hand lip of this cave marked by a huge hanging root of ivy.

① Bag of X   F6c+

12m A poor route. From right-hand side of cave, climb the wall above to a difficult finale.
Gary Gibson, Nadim Siddiqui, 1995

② X Marks the Spot   F5

10m A much easier line to the right of the huge hanging bush. Pleasant.
Nadim Siddiqui, 1995

③ eXit Stage Left   F6a

11m A pleasant shallow groove rising from the centre of the platform.
Nadim Siddiqui, 1995

④ The X Files   F6b+

11m A tricky lower bulge just to the right.
Nadim Siddiqui, 1995

⑤ eXtra Time   F6b+

11m The left-hand of two lines from the bolt belay at the end of the ledge.
Nadim Siddiqui, 1995

⑥ Red X   ★   F6c

11m The best route from the terrace takes the right-hand side of the wall above the bolt belay. Good sustained climbing.
Nadim Siddiqui, 1995

The next routes begin from where the approach path reaches the first section of crag proper. This is 8m to the right of a broken wall.

⑦ Great Expectations   ★   F6c

15m Varied face climbing via the prominent hanging slab. Watch out for the finish which provides the inevitable sting in the tail.
Nadim Siddiqui, 1995

⑧ Certificate X   ★ ★   F7b

15m A fine pitch. Easy climbing leads to the first break. Hard moves lead left through the scoop to a fingery and trying finale. Clipping the last bolt is the crux!
Nadim Siddiqui, 1995

⑨ Malcolm X   ★   F7a+

15m Takes a rightwards exit from Certificate X involving good moves on hollow holds.
Nadim Siddiqui, 1995

⑩ Top MarX ★ **F7a**

12m The steep wall to the right again. Hard moves above the break which are best done quickly.
Gary Gibson, Nadim Siddiqui, 1995

⑪ XXXX ★ ★ **F7b**

12m The best route on the crag, climbing the compact grey wall above the break. Fine, sustained wall climbing and low in the grade.
Nadim Siddiqui, 1995

⑫ Little Blue Lies ★ **F7b**

12m High in the grade. The wall to the right yields only to a positive approach.
Gary Gibson, 1995

⑬ Y Should I ★ **F7b+**

12m Hard moves through the bulge to the right precede a difficult move onto the slab. Hard to on-sight.
Gary Gibson, Nadim Siddiqui, 1995

⑭ Xcursion **F7c+**

11m A totally hideous problem through the bulge and up through the scoop above. Belay on the right.
Gary Gibson, 1997

⑮ X.T.C. **F7a+**

10m A short, hard and innocuous crux over the bulge at the right-hand side of the cliff.
Gary Gibson, 1995

Smalldale

O.S. Ref. **SK097771**   Altitude: **310m a.s.l.**

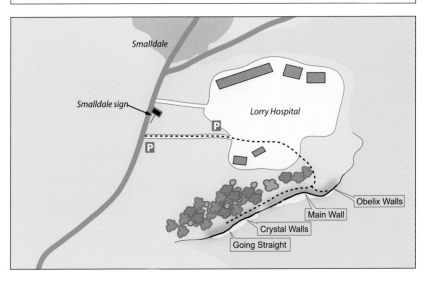

This large quarry, which has only recently reached its full potential, must now lay claim to being one of the best of its type in the Peak. Fine steep wall climbs abound with a large quota of routes in the F7 grades. Recent developments have made the cliff more accessible to the middle-grade sport climber operating in the mid F6s grade with a few easier grade climbs thrown in for good measure.

The crag's setting can seem unpleasant and off-putting at first, as the approach involves walking through a works yard specialising in the repair of busses and lorries, and a huffing and puffing that comes from mysterious sheds at the back of the yard makes it sound like thay also do a bit of work on the odd dragon. However, while this may not be solitude and natural beauty, it is, like many of the quarries in this guide, another unique setting. The owner of the yard is friendly, although he does think climbers are mad. Be sure to make him aware of your arrival.

The climbing

Over 40 routes, mainly in the F6 range, but with a dozen high-quality F7s. All long single pitch, up to 20m high, on good quality rock. The routes are mainly wall climbs, but many are based around arêtes and cracks, giving them good variety and a lot of character.

Traditional climbs

The crag has had a handful of traditional climbs added over the years, mainly taking the major crack-lines. See main introduction for more details.

Conditions & aspect

The cliff faces north-west and only gets any evening sunlight from roughly 4pm onwards. In the wintertime this can be a cold and inhospitable place but in the summer months it provides a welcome retreat from any cliffs roasting in warm sunshine or provides an ideal evening venue. Seepage does affect the main wall after rain but does not affect routes too adversely in the summer months.

Parking & approach

This relatively large quarry lies on the outskirts of Buxton in the small village of the same name on the road between Dove Holes and Peak Forest. Its position should make it easily accessible for all Peak District climbers.

When travelling north out of Buxton along the A6 pass the golf course and after 1km take a right turn for Batham Gate - this point can be reached by travelling south through Dove Holes and after 2km reaching the same point. Follow this route through Peak Dale and into Smalldale where the quarry will be evident on the right-hand side of the road. Alternatively, when travelling along the A623 from Stoney Middleton, take a left turn opposite the Devonshire Arms in Peak Forest. Follow this road past a 90 degree bend into Smalldale after 3km.

From just outside the village, a gravel track leads into the quarry. Do not park on this road but on the next tarmacadam road leading to the brick works. Walk through the small lorry park below the crag to reach it - please treat the owner with a degree of courtesy and inform him of your presence. He is friendly, although due to break ins he has had to acquire a rather large dog, and in his own words, "There's nothing that dog likes more than to tear a few lumps out of you!"

From the parking, the routes can be accessed in 2 minutes by walking across the yard and carefully crossing the fence in the corner.

Obelix Walls

To the left of the prominent white Main Wall the cliff slants up and to the left and forms a cliff at right angles with a grassy bank running below it. Where this levels out a tier of rock runs leftwards to form a smaller cliff of good rock.

Obelix Walls

The main, left-facing part of the wall is east-facing and only receives sunshine in the morning hours of summer. The smaller area at the top gets some evening sun.

❶ The Ladybird Killers   **F6c**
9m A short route at left-hand of terrace. Technical.
Gary Gibson, Jim Burton, 1995

❷ Six Bee or Not Six Bee   **F6c+**
9m The harder and more technical right-hand twin. You decide the grade?
Gary Gibson, Jim Burton, 1995

❸ Terry and June   **F6c**
11m This route takes the wall 20m to the left of the top of the slope. Follow a thin crack to an intricate finish.
Gary Gibson, 1986

❹ Squawkietawkie   **F7a**
11m The sharp-edged arête at the top of and facing down the slope. A difficult entry via twin overlaps leads to a delicate climax.
Gary Gibson, Jim Burton, 1995

Obelix Walls

5 Obelix ★ F7a+

12m The impressive grey tower at the top of the slope is taken centrally. Fingery climbing with some intricate final moves.
Gary Gibson, 1995

6 Getafix ★ F7b

15m The right-hand arête of the tower is airy above a box-shaped recess and difficult in its top half. Well worth seeking out and low in the grade.
Gary Gibson, Jim Burton, 1995

7 Play it Again, Sam HVS 5a

16m The major square-cut corner is followed by bridging and jamming.
Senan Hennessy, 1985

8 Reservoir Frogs ★ ★ F6c

18m The first route on the wall when approaching from below. An excellent introduction to wall climbing with the main difficulties concentrated within the first 12m.
Gary Gibson, Jim Burton, 1995

The Main Wall

The gleaming white wall is the showpiece of the cliff and provides a number of fine, sustained wall climbs. This is not an ideal winter venue but a perfect one for a summer evening or one of those sultry summer days we so often get in Britain.

The wall faces north-west, takes little seepage and receives any sunshine that is going after 5pm.

9 First Offence ★ ★ F7a

18m The impressive arête dividing the two walls. Superb climbing in a fine position and requiring a long reach at the crux.
Bob Conway, 1985

10 When Reason Sleeps ★ ★ F7a+

18m Low in the grade but just deserves it after the start and a bold section at mid-height. The walls right of the arête provide the entertainment. First-rate climbing on the upper walls.
Gary Gibson, 1995

The Main Wall

11 **Stainsby Girls** ★ **F7a+**

15m The wall 8m right of the arête contains an angled overlap. Gain this directly via an elongated gash and follow it to a trying exit. An old classic, yet a little disappointing compared to its neighbours.
Chris Jackson, 1985 / Gary Gibson, Jim Burton, 1995

12 **Virtual Insanity** ★ ★ **F7b**

18m Superb fingery climbing aiming for a left-facing flake at 12m. Started direct and culminating in a slightly disappointing finish on the arête, the only drawback on an otherwise great climb.
Nadim Siddiqui, Gary Gibson, Jim Burton, 1995

13 **Soft Centre** ★ **F7a+**

18m A poorly-bolted pitch slap bang up the centre of the face via a shallow groove in a black streak. Gaining the overlap proves to be the crux. Above the overlap, the groove gives easier climbing to a steep finish.
Jim Burton, Gary Gibson, Nadim Siddiqui, 1995

14 **Lies and Deception** ★ **F7a**

18m The smooth-looking wall gives fine climbing to the overlap. Once above this, follow the wall to the right of the groove with a baffling crux move.
Gary Gibson, Jim Burton, 1995

15 **Lost Contact** ★ ★ ★ **F7a+**

18m A great pitch, low in the grade. The shallow, left-facing groove and thin crack above give airy and sustained climbing towards the top.
Bill Wintrip, 1985

16 **Soggy Biscuits** ★ ★ ★ **F7b+**

18m Another brilliant pitch taking the wall and vague pillar. Steep and sustained climbing leads to a final difficult sequence above the penultimate bolt.
Simon Lee, 1990s

17 **Can Boys** ★ ★ **F7a**

18m A sustained and fingery face climb, beginning as for the last route but continuing direct. A little bold for some modern tastes.
Neil Foster, 1986

**Right: Nadim 'Sid' Siddiqui on Virtual Insanity (opposite page). F7b.
Photo: David Simmonite.**

⓲ Bedlam   **F6c+**
12m The final route of the wall, started high on the right, gives a blind and sportingly bolted pitch. Good face climbing despite this.
Gary Gibson, Jim Burton, 1995

The Crystal Walls

Situated 80m right of the main crag is a series of walls of good quality limestone. These have recently provided a fine supply of routes in the F6 grades. The first set of walls is terminated by a gully on its left-hand side and a prominent wide crack, complete with cave, to its right. These walls receive evening sunshine and do not suffer major seepage problems in the summer months. The rock is generally compact with the occasional friable hold.

The routes are described from left to right starting with two isolated routes at a higher level and only 50m to the right of the Main Wall.

If you are leaving Smalldale on a sunny late summer evening, stop your car and check out the beautiful flooded quarry lying just up the hill before Peak Dale (see Buxton Area map). In the late evening light, flocks of heron flying around the bull-rushes amid the amazing golden water is a sight that will gladden the heart of any nature lover.

The next route begins the first of a series on the long walls 30m to the right.

㉑ Fringe Meeting   **F6a**
10m The small isolated wall just left of the gully system. A short crux section low down.
Gary Gibson, Nick Taylor, 2002

㉒ Own Biddy Flogger   **F6a**
11m The right arête of the gully. Pleasant high up.
Gary Gibson, Andy Beaumont, Nick Taylor, 2002

㉓ The Crystal Maze   ★ **F6c+**
15m Sustained, technical face climbing to the right. Blind moves throughout with a particularly trying and climactic finale. Easier after viewing the holds from the next route!
Gary & Hazel Gibson, 1995

⓳ Bolt 45   **F6a+**
6m The left-hand line has spaced bolt runners.
Jim Campbell, Keith Ashton, Harry Venables, 1997

⓴ Bosch Spice   **F6b**
6m Again sportingly bolted, the right-hand and better of the pair.
Keith Ashton, Jim Campbell, Harry Venables, 1997

23 24 21 22 25 26 27 28 29 30 31 32
Crystal Walls

24 Hollow Inside   F6b

15m A comparable route to the last climb, although much easier. Climb the face to the right passing an obvious ledge and flake. The finish, via the technical rib, leads to a step left and the belay of the last route.
Gary & Hazel Gibson, 1996

25 The Quartz Tricycle   ★   F6b+

18m This route gives sustained wall climbing with a difficult start and a finish up the centre of the upper tower.
Gary & Hazel Gibson, 1995

26 Friezian   F6b

18m A hard technical start leads to easier climbing slightly rightwards to gain the belay. High in the grade.
Gary Gibson, Nick Taylor, 2002

27 Lady Luck   ★   F6a+

18m Another pleasant route on good rock. Again the difficulties lie in the first 10m. After this swing right and up via a pleasant face and impressive quartz thread.
Gary Gibson, Nick Taylor, 2002

28 Just Passing Through   ★ F6a

18m Another agreeable pitch. A direct line right of the obvious wide crack / chimney to a difficult finale. Can you pass through the cave? Only slim Jims need apply.
Gary Gibson, Nick Taylor, 2002

29 Sock It To 'em   ★ ★ F5

18m Great rock and climbing. Takes a direct line just left of the prominent wide crack dividing the buttresses. Nowhere difficult.
Gary Gibson, Nick Taylor, 2002

SMALLDALE
Please drive slowly

Crystal Walls
30 31 32 33 34 35 36 37 38

Going Straight Wall

The larger set of walls to the right provides longer and better routes. A great place to climb in the summer months since sunshine glints the walls from 4pm onwards. The rock is also more compact but most of the routes feel a little sporting on first acquaintance.

30 Stone the Crows ★ F6b
20m This is the first line to the right of the wide fissure. A series of cracks and a wall lead to the 'crows nest'. The final tower provides the finely-positioned finish.
Gary Gibson, Nick Taylor, 2002

31 Learn the Lingo ★ ★ F6c
20m A long sustained pitch on the left edge of the wall. Not too hard but makes the grade due to the blind nature of the climbing.
Gary Gibson, 2002

32 Mr Love Pants ★ F6b+
18m The right-hand branch from Learn the Lingo. Again fine rock and climbing sticking direct to the line of bolt runners.
Gary Gibson, 2002

33 Shanacie ★ ★ F6b
20m Great climbing; direct, sustained and satisfying to finish up the obvious crack. Hardest low down.
Senan Hennessy, 1985 / Gary Gibson, 2002

34 Riding the Bullet ★ ★ F6c
20m A fine companion route to Shanacie. Again, difficult low down when taken direct and this time with a fine climax on the headwall.
Gary Gibson, Andy Beaumont, Nick Taylor, 2002

35 More Chattery Teeth ★ F6b
20m Pleasant climbing with a steep start. Enjoyable face climbing then leads to a steep finish via a crack.
Gary Gibson, Jim Burton, 2003

Crystal Walls

38 39 40 41 42 43

41 **Single Decker** **F6a+**
9m A very short route on the right-hand side of the wall. One hard move.
Gary Gibson, 2003

42 **Triple Sec** **F6b**
20m An easy wall leads to a ledge- care with rock here. The difficult wall above has worryingly hollow holds. The final pillar gives pleasant enough climbing if you get that far!
Gary Gibson, Nick Taylor, 2002

43 **Double Wammy** **F6b+**
20m A route tackling both tiers. The steep lower wall is mainly juggy. The upper wall gives fine climbing to a difficult finish, taken direct.
Gary Gibson, 2002

36 **Open Season** ★ **F6b**
15m A tricky lower wall leads to steep jug pulling to gain the belay.
Gary Gibson, Andy Beaumont, Nick Taylor, 2002

37 **Upminster Kid** **F6b**
20m The poorest route on this section of rock. Ascend the wall and slim tower using holds slightly left. Swing right to join Going Straight before the final tower.
Gary Gibson, Nick Taylor, 2002

38 **Going Straight** ★ ★ **F6c**
20m Superb clean rock and fine sustained climbing lead to a finish up the tower.
Bob Conway, 1985

39 **Friend 15** **F6a+**
15m Direct climbing via a box-shaped recess and the odd fragile hold. Sportingly bolted.
Chris Jackson, 1985

40 **Shame on You** **F6b**
15m Direct climbing via a short ramp and steep little wall. Worthwhile.
Gary Gibson, Nick Taylor, 2002

Harpur Hill

O.S. Ref. **SK065708**   Altitude: **345m a.s.l.**

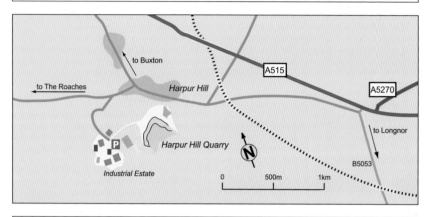

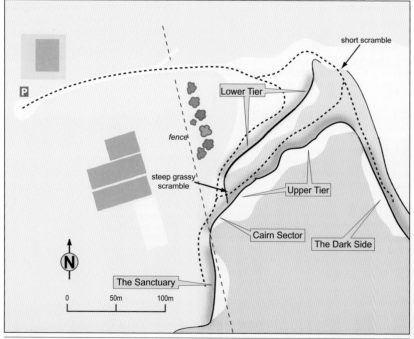

Much has been written over the past few years of the climbing at Harpur Hill, the majority of which has centred on the argument over sport climbing. The quarry has had a long tradition of aid climbs and naturally protected routes since the 1960s, with a particularly healthy year in 1986. In 1994 Nadim Siddiqui and Bill Birch began redevelopment of the quarry with a view to providing a major sport climbing venue for the area with routes throughout the grading spectrum. Of course, such actions were to raise a few eyebrows and during the ensuing debate the majority of the bolts were stripped from the routes and the venue was no more.

Subsequent to this, and after a somewhat heated debate, it was agreed that sport climbing could coexist alongside the traditional routes of the crag as long as bolts were not placed to conflict with these routes. Hence a large number of routes have been rebolted and a significant number of new routes added.

Due to this, this cliff now proves to be one of the best and most popular of its type in the area with a host of routes in the low- to mid-grades. They reach up to a maximum height of 25m on a variety of excellent rock types from that of the typically quarried of the lower tier through to the extremely abrasive on the upper tier where the quarrying has exposed large tracts of varied, calcite-encrusted rock almost natural in nature.

The climbing

Harpur Hill stands second only to Horseshoe Quarry in the number, range and quality of its mid-grade sport climbing. Almost 150 climbs with a great spread catering for all grades up to the low F7s. All single pitch, although 2 pitch experiences are on offer by combining routes. Climbs are all vertical or off-vertical walls, arêtes, grooves corners and cracks. Mostly quarried, but the upper uier especially is well-weathered to produce a near natural limestone feel.

Traditional climbs

There are almost 60 traditionally protected climbs in the quarry. These were mainly added in the mid 1980s, although many more were added at the time of the bolting controversy in the mid 1990s. Only the most significant are noted here. For further information, see the main introduction.

Conditions & aspect

The main upper and lower tier routes have been supplemented, in recent years, with new additions found on the Dark Side and Sanctuary areas. Due to their orientation, north-east and south-west respectively, this means that there are crags here that will receive whatever sun or shelter there is going. The main faces face north-west, and get the sun later in the day. The crag can be windy, but again, shelter can often be found.

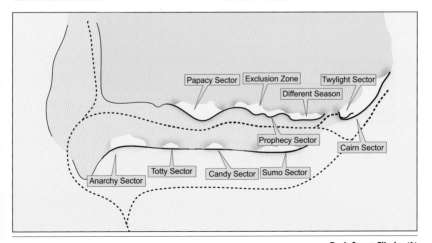

Approaches

This has to be one of the most conspicuous quarries in the Peak District, standing clearly on the edge of Buxton and easily seen when approaching from the west.

A small subsidiary road arcs off to the left of the main A515 Ashbourne to Buxton road at Brierlow Bar and leads to the village of Harpur Hill. Take a left turn opposite the church and as the road descends the hill take a left turn into Harpur Hill industrial estate. Alternatively, take the first right turn at Burbidge on the A52 Leek to Buxton road and follow this subsidiary road down a steep hill: the right turn here leads into the industrial estate. Follow this road past a sharp left-hand bend and where the road takes a sharp right park here alongside some orange gates. Walk past the gates along the gravel track into the lower tier of the quarry.

Note: Parking is limited in this area and there have been instances of security guards taking particular offence to the number of cars that may be left here. For this reason please park carefully.

The Lower Tier

The lower tier is the first rock encountered upon entering the quarry. Although the routes might lack definition and stature compared to those on the upper tier, their friendly nature makes them a good starting point. Routes begin with an isolated arête 30m left of the obvious black wall.

Anarchy Sector

Situated in the far left-hand end of the lower tier this area offers a compact grey wall with excellent rock and a couple of titbits to their left. Receives very little sunshine until the evening. The cliff can also have a very damp base after rain.

① Overbored   **F5**
9m   The short arête with an impressive borehole.
Gary & Hazel Gibson, Nadim Siddiqui, 2001

② Getting the Groove   **F6a**
12m   The lone groove further right, starting with an awkward corner.
Gary & Hazel Gibson, Nadim Siddiqui, 2001

③ Mine Anarchy   **F6a**
12m   The pillar and wall above on sloping holds, all on the main black wall.
Gary & Hazel Gibson, Nadim Siddiqui, 2001

④ Only Ken's Anarchy Will Do   **F6b**
11m   Climb direct to the left-hand side a of small overlap. Technical between the 1st and 2nd bolts.
Gary & Hazel Gibson, Nadim Siddiqui, 2001

Anarchy Sector

Gary Gibson on The Talisman, F7a
(page 133). Photo: Carl Ryan.

Candy Sector

⑤ Always Break the Rules ★ F5+
10m A direct line to the right with sustained moves on perfect rock.
Gary & Hazel Gibson, Nadim Siddiqui, 2001

⑥ Snap Decision F5
11m The right-hand side of the wall moving left to reach the belay.
Gary & Hazel Gibson, Nadim Siddiqui, 2001

Candy Sector

A longer section of wall with a handful of better routes. A place to tick a lot in a very short space of time although some routes may feel very similar. Again evening sun only and dries relatively quickly. Not a winter venue.

⑦ The Candy Man ★ F6a+
11m The final calcite-ridden slab gives an agreeable route, much like its right-hand twin.
Gary & Hazel Gibson, Gordon Jenkin, 2001

⑧ Flossy's Slab ★ F6a+
11m Pleasant slab climbing on the calcite to the right.
Gary & Hazel Gibson, Gordon Jenkin, 2001

⑨ Toy Story F6a
11m Easier climbing from the left-hand side of a pancake of rock leads rightwards to the belay.
Gary Gibson, 2001

⑩ Suck on This F6a+
10m Strike direct through the obvious ledge system to climb the wall above. Hard starting moves.
Gary Gibson, 2001

⑪ Smartie People are Happy People F6a
10m The centre of the pleasant black wall with enjoyable moves. Can be made harder by sticking strictly to the line of bolts.
Gordon Jenkin, Gary Gibson, 2001

⑫ Candy Store F6a
10m This climb takes the right-hand arête of the obvious black wall.
Gordon Jenkin, Gary & Hazel Gibson, 2001

A prominent crack lies just to the right. The next route starts just right of this.

⑬ Tempting Children F6c+
11m Climb the difficult hanging groove above the ledge to the right.
Gary Gibson, Gordon Jenkin, Nadim Siddiqui, 2001

⑭ Would you like a Sweety ★ F6c

11m The best route on the sector. Climb direct via the slabby wall and overlap.
Gary Gibson, Nadim Siddiqui, Gordon Jenkin, 2001

⑮ Bolts R Us F6a+

11m The arête to the right taken on its left-hand side and finishing via the face above. Worthwhile.
Gary Gibson, Nadim Siddiqui, Gordon Jenkin, 2001

⑯ Sing for Your Dinner F6b+

11m From the base of a depression to the right trend leftwards across the wall.
Gary Gibson, 2001

Totty Sector

A nondescript wall in the centre of the lower tier. It offers a handful of easier routes and can be identified by a small, round cave at its foot. Again, only evening sun with a little seepage after wet weather.

Totty Sector

⑰ A Bit of Totty F6a

12m Climb a short pillar and the steeper wall above. The best route on this section of cliff.
Gary & Hazel Gibson, 2001

⑱ Top Totty F5+

12m A leftwards-rising line with sustained climbing.
Gary Gibson, 2001

⑲ Jelly Tots F4+

9m The easy thin crack in centre of wall.
Gary & Hazel Gibson, 2001

⑳ Tiny Tots F5

11m The better, left-hand, of two lines via a scoop.
Gary & Hazel Gibson, 2001

㉑ Teeny Tots F5

11m The rightmost line of the wall keeping to the rib.
Gary & Hazel Gibson, 2001

Sumo Sector

Situated towards the right-hand side of the lower tier and opposite to the entrance into the quarry, this area gives a broad selection of routes in the lower sport climbing grades and two tastier and harder morsels. The wall dries quickly and gets the evening sun.

㉒ The Jap's Eyes are on You F6b+

10m The first tricky wall keeping leftwards on the upper section.
Gary Gibson, 2001

㉓ Outside Tokyo F6b

12m Start up the leftwards-facing flake and go over the bulge. From the ledge easier climbing ensues.
Gary Gibson, 2001

㉔ Nagasaki Grooves 2 F6b

12m The groove and flake line with an awkward bulge provides the right-hand start. Hardly a comparison to its namesake?
Gary & Hazel Gibson, 2001

㉕ Sumo ★ F7a

12m Hard, technical climbing. Keep to the overhung blunt arête to the right. Easier climbing from the ledge leads to the belay.
Gary Gibson, 2001

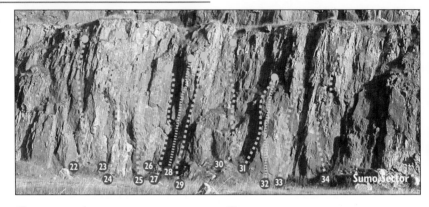

26 A Nip in the Air   **F6b**

11m The thin crack in the left wall of the obvious corner gives a sporting finale.
Gary & Hazel Gibson, 2001

27 Geisha Grooves   **F6a**

11m The corner-line with good moves. Exit left to the belay.
Gary & Hazel Gibson, 2001

28 Saweno Gancho   ★ **F6c+**

12m The vague arête to the right has blind and fingery moves.
Gary Gibson, 2001

29 Setting Son   **F6a**

11m The enjoyable shallow groove.
Gary Gibson, 2001

30 The Golden Goose   **F5**

12m A longer and easier route over ledgy ground to the right.
Gary Gibson, 2002

31 Hong Kong Fewy   **F6a+**

9m One hard move on the left-hand wall of a low-level rib.
Gary Gibson, 2002

32 The Rising Sun   **F5+**

9m Another short route via the blunt arête, with a hard initial move. Perfect rock.
Gary Gibson, 2001

33 Kamikaze Clone   **F6a+**

11m Climb the right-hand side a of a low-level rib, then the right-hand side of the short arête above.
Gary & Hazel Gibson, 2001

34 Riding Shogun   **F6b**

12m An isolated pillar to the right of the main section of the face.
Gary & Hazel Gibson, 2001

Cairn Sector

Undoubtedly the best section of the lower tier, this area of crag can be found at its right-hand end. It contains one of the cliff's classics in the form of a striking, eyelash flake and a number of other worthy routes. A number of easier routes originally bolted have yet to be re-geared - it remains to be seen whether they ever will be.

A superb place to visit for an evening although showing signs of popularity.

These walls dry very quickly, catch any wind that's going but receive the sun's rays from about 2.30pm onwards in the summer months.

35 The Misfits   **F6a**

15m The left-hand route, taking a pillar and short headwall. Limited quality.
Gary Gibson, Jim Burton, 2002

36 Hissin' Sid F6b

15m A slightly better route taking a difficult overlap and the pleasant wall above.
Bill Birch, Nadim Siddiqui (both led), 1994

37 Slippery Bill HVS 5a

15m A vague shallow groove line.
R Hyde, Bill Birch (both led), 1994

38 Ratline ★ ★ F7b+

12m A desperately thin, thin crack-line. May seem easier on a redpoint but does not on-sight! Superb moves.
Nadim Siddiqui, Bill Birch, 1994

39 Cairn ★ ★ ★ F6c+

12m A true classic taking the prominent angled flake. Gaining it and finishing direct provides the main difficulties.
Nadim Siddiqui, Bill Birch, 1994

40 Stealth ★ ★ F7a

12m A variant from the very top of the flake. Quite fine, but you will have to withstand the pains of a very sharp pocket.
Nadim Siddiqui, Bill Birch, 1994

41 Great White ★ F5+

12m Pleasant slab climbing above the overlap. Orca F6b (Bill Birch, Rick Gibbon, 1996) climbs direct through this.
Bill Birch, Nadim Siddiqui (both led), 1994

42 The Naked Spur ★ F4+

12m Another very pleasant pitch up the sharp right-hand arête of the slab.
Gary Gibson, Jim Burton, 2002

43 Assault and Battery F6b+

10m A short fingery exercise in the back of the bay.
Gary Gibson, Jim Burton, 2002

44 Trial and Error F7a

10m The overhanging arête proves difficult for 5m of its length. Good moves.
Nadim Siddiqui, Bill Birch, 1994

45 Senile Delinquents F5

15m A prominent flake and crack-line finishing via an overlap.
Bill Birch, Nadim Siddiqui (both led), 1994

46 Cabin Fever F6b

15m The wall to the right provides a tight squeeze with one hard move.
Keith Bridgens, 2003

The final routes on this sector lie on a small wall 10m to the right.

47 Breakfast at Safeways F6b

10m The left-hand side of the slab. Becoming a little slippery, and with a high first bolt.
Bill Birch, Nadim Siddiqui (both led), 1994

48 99p Special   F6a+
10m Marginally easier starting via a thin crack. Soon eases above. The crack itself is a very enjoyable climb (**Jam Butty Mines Crack,** VS 4c ★).
Bill Birch, Nadim Siddiqui (both led), 1994

49 Food for Sport   F6a
10m The pleasant right arête of the wall.
Bill Birch, Nadim Siddiqui (both led), 1994

Upper Tier

This is gained by either of two scrambles, one going up left of the first routes on the lower tier, the other up the steep grassy banking left of Cairn Sector.

Papacy Buttress

The first developed buttress on the cliff both traditionally and as a sport climbing venue, this face is situated in the centre of the upper tier. Long routes abound in the mid to high F6s with a very pleasant feeling of exposure accompanying them.

Many of the arguments that surrounded the bolting debate over Harpur Hill centred around routes on Papacy Buttress. Most of the routes on the front of the face were led on natural protection subsequent to them having their bolts removed, with Apollo Creed and Rocky Variations giving two superb E3 leads. Some bolts were then put back into some routes. A level of mutual respect was eventually arrived at, however, as both sides have ultimately accepted a level of bolting and debolting, and both styles now exist on the cliff.

The right-hand side of the face receives the sunshine from around 2.30pm in the summer months but can feel uncomfortably cold in breezy conditions.

1 This England   F7a+
12m This takes the hard blank-looking face with fingery moves, where a long reach helps.
Gary Gibson, 1998

2 Grit Arête   ★   F7a
12m Defined by name. Very rough rock and unusually rounded moves on the blunt arête.
Gary Gibson, Paul Harrison, 1998

❸ Strangled at Birth ★ F6c
l4m Rarely repeated, although worth seeking out. Tucked away with fine face moves on the black face.
Gary Gibson, Paul Harrison, 1998

The remainder of the routes lie on the front face, and provide a good number of quality challenges.

❹ Seven Deadly Sins HVS 5a
18m A classic trad line.
Bob Toogood, Bob Dearman, 1966

❺ Coral Seas ★ ★ F6a
18m A wandering line with much merit. Take the initial rib direct before transferring left. A tricky bulge then leads to a rightwards exit across the finely positioned slab.
Bill Birch, Nadim Siddiqui (both led), 1994

❻ Avarice Allsorts ★ ★ F6c
18m The roofs that Coral Seas avoids taken head on. The upper arête is superb.
Gary Gibson, Dave Law, 1998

*The next routes lie right of the wide crack (**Lust**, VS 4b, Bob Dearman & party, 1966). Other traditionally protected routes exist on the buttress, and are worth checking out. See introduction for further details.*

❼ Rocky Variations ★ ★ F6b+
20m The left-hand of two very fine pitches beginning atop a grey block to the right of the wide crack splitting the face. Sustained, though never hard. Exit the scoop on the left and take the overhang above on the right.
Bill Birch, Nadim Siddiqui (both led), 1994

❽ Apollo Creed ★ ★ F6b
20m The right-hand twin provides a harder move exiting the right-hand side of the scoop. More rests and breathers accompany this route.
Bill Birch, Nadim Siddiqui, 1994

*To the right is a tall, capped groove. This is taken by **Seven Deally Virtues**, HVS 5b (Grahem West, Brian Roberts, early 1960s), which gains the groove from the left, and avoids the capping overhang by going right. The cracked overhang direct is a superb E3 6a.*

❾ Full Frontal ★ ★ F6c
22m A great route taking the central pillar of the face. Most avoid the direct start (F6c+?) by utilising the groove on the right. There is then a mid-height crux.
Nadim Siddiqui, Bill Birch, 1994

❿ Power of Soul ★ ★ F7b+
18m A faint, thin crack to the right of the main groove-line. Very hard moves past the third bolt runner gain a break and marginally easier moves above. Needs cool conditions and is graded for an on-sight.
Nadim Siddiqui, Bill Birch, Jim Burton, 1994

⓫ Dementia Normale F6a
18m A way of not doing Power of Soul on-sight. A pleasant crack and groove to its right leads eventually by leftwards moves to its belay.
Gary Gibson, 1998

⓬ The Last Straw F6b
18m Appropriately named. A thin crack system on the right-hand wall of the buttress is hardest low down.
Gary Gibson, Gordon Jenkin, 2001

⓭ Figure of Law ★ F7a
l5m A hidden gem taking the towering wall at the top of the gully on the right-hand side of the buttress. Hard above the third bolt runner.
Gary Gibson, Dave Law, 1998

Exclusion Zone Buttress

The cliff loses its height for a while until, in about 50m, it returns to its full scale at a prominent corner system. The side-walls of this provide an array of longer routes in the mid F6s. The wall containing Exclusion Zone is the first to receive any sunshine on the upper tier - about 2pm. Again the rock is of good quality quarried limestone on the bolted routes.

14 Cool Danny   F6b
12m Tackle the strip overhang direct to reach the face above.
Gary Gibson, 1998

15 Screaming Wheels   ★ F6b+
15m A finely positioned arête taken direct at the start. Keep to the arête higher up. Named after the local race track.
Gary Gibson, 1998

16 No Man's Land   F6c
18m The left-hand branch off Exclusion Zone with a bouldery start and harder finale. Can be mossy high up so take a look from the top of its neighbour.
Gary Gibson, 1999

17 Exclusion Zone   ★ ★ F6b+
18m The centre of the west-facing wall gives a superb, sporty pitch; take a wire or two if you feel nervous, and take care clipping the first bolt.
Gary Gibson, 1998

18 Iron Curtain   ★ F6b
18m An easier alternative to the last route with pleasant sustained moves leading to a steep finale. Not quite as fine, but still very worthwhile.
Gary & Hazel Gibson, 1999

19 Mouse Hunt   ★ F6c
18m The right-hand wall of the bay and starting just to the left of an elderberry tree. A hard starting bulge and excellent, though run-out, upper wall.
Gary Gibson, 1998

20 Thing Thang   F7a
11m The better of two short routes to the right. Technical and worth doing.
Gary Gibson, 1998

21 Thang Thing   F7a
11m The right-hand, poorer line for puerile tickers only. Exit the wide crack a.s.a.p.
Gary Gibson, 1998

**Rick Gibbon on In The Gravy, F6a
(page 133). Photo: Niall Grimes.**

Slab de Lune   F6a+
12m A poor slab route, shown by the return of its vegetation. Mid-height difficulties.
Gary Gibson, 2001

Sack of Stones   ★ F6b
12m A hard start if taken direct. Easier above with a fluttery finish.
Gary & Hazel Gibson, 1998

Bag of Bones   ★ ★ F6a+
15m A sustained face climb just left of a hammer-head block. Excellent.
Gary & Hazel Gibson, 1998

Sara Laughs   F6b
15m A technical wall above the centre of the lower ledge system.
Gary Gibson, 1998

Calci Mauve   ★ F6b
20m A long Portlandesque route beginning up the front face of a pillar, building up to a very fine finish on beautiful calcite-covered rock. Avoid the wide crack on the right.
Gary Gibson, 1998

Glas Double   F7a
20m The desperately fingery right-hand variant.
Gary Gibson, 1999

Prophecy Buttress

This long area of cliff contains a myriad of varied climbs and features. Towards its left-hand side a series of excellent slabs offer a number of easier routes reminiscent of Staden Quarry. A long, though vague corner running the full height of the crag marks the central section. Either side of this lie this cliff's best routes. On a fine summer evening you can be setting off on your last route at gone 10pm and the Traveller's Rest lies only 5km away. What pleasure! The rock is excellent with a number of routes featuring a superb blend of quartz-encrusted rock with the highest friction levels.

The cliff receives sunshine from late afternoon.

Over the Hill   ★ ★ F6c
18m A classic thin crack climb leads to an overlap from where good, open face moves lead to the top.
Gary Gibson, Gordon Jenkin, 2001

㉙ Nostalgia ★ **E4 6a**

22m The snaking thin crack system to the right gives a classic traditional route worthy of attention. May be bolted by the time you read this. F6c+.
Gary Gibson, 1998

㉚ Yogi Bear ★ **F7a**

18m The blackened face to the right with intricate moves on hidden holds. The face above is taken just to the left of the bolts. Easier for the tall.
Gary Gibson, 1998

㉛ Four Telling Tales ★ ★ **F6c**

18m Thin crack and left-hand side of arête. Balance and friction climbing at their best.
Gary Gibson, 1998

㉜ The Talisman ★ **F7a**

18m The right-hand side of the arête. Hard above the third bolt with 'barn-door' moves to gain Four Telling Tales.
Gary Gibson, 1998

㉝ The Oracle ★ **F7b**

11m Super-technical face climbing following a line of silver hangers and not many holds.
Gary Gibson, 1998

㉞ The Prophecy ★ ★ **F7a**

20m The original route of the wall and a classic if the line is adhered to. The lower wall is taken direct on the line of bolts. A hard bulge and long reach gain the break. The upper arête is taken direct and is fairly 'out there'.
Gary Gibson, 1998

㉟ The Indian Cottage **F6c+**

12m A green arête and blocky overlap to the right provide two good moves.
Gary Gibson, 1998

㊱ Aloo Gobi **F6c**

11m A short hard route via an overlap and wall.
Gary Gibson, 1999

㊲ Pappadum Groove **F6a**

9m A short shallow groove of little quality.
Gary Gibson, 1998

㊳ Quartz Initial **F6b**

9m A one move wonder up the very short arête to the right.
Gary Gibson, 1998

㊴ Viagra Falls ★ **F6c+**

15m A hard start over the bulge to the left of the thin crack leads to enjoyable face climbing right of the flake. The upper overlap provides a thuggy finale.
Gary Gibson, 1998

㊵ Different Season ★ **F6a**

15m The thin crack-line with an airy start. Agreeably sustained.
Gary Gibson, 1998

㊶ Apt Pupil ★ **F6c**

18m Escalating difficulties on the lower face right of the crack lead to a trying overlap and airy moves to gain the belay.
Gary Gibson, 1998

㊷ In the Gravy ★ **F6a**

20m A long pitch utilising the summit of the pinnacle and enjoyable face climbing above.
Gary Gibson, 1998

㊸ From Cradle to Grave ★ **F6c**

20m The side-wall left of the corner. Taken direct, especially at the top, this gives a route high its grade. Slinking off left does not count.
Gary Gibson, 1998

㊹ Calcite Claws ★ **F6c**

11m A great little pitch which belies its length. Take the arête to the right head on.
Gary Gibson, 1998

㊺ So Veneer **F6b**

11m Two difficult moves on the right-hand side of the arête lead to the same belay.
Gary Gibson, 1999

㊻ The End **F6a**

9m Appropriately named in all senses. Hard at the start.
Gary Gibson, Gordon Jenkin, 2001

Twilight Sector

This is the section of cliff above the path leading to the upper tier. It gives a mixture of reasonable routes with one of significant quality. It receives the sun from about 3pm onwards in the summer months and all of the routes are on excellent rock.

47 Inconsiderate Blinking   **F6a+**
11m Situated on the left-hand fringe of the wall is this obvious arête gained via a tricky start.
Gary Gibson, Nick Taylor, 2002

48 Unilateral Thinking   **F6c**
12m A short, steep wall and vague arête to its right complete with an array of calcite features.
Gary Gibson, Andy Grondowski, 1999

49 The Light   ★ **F7a**
12m Fine climbing. The centre of the white wall to the right with hard moves and an exposed feel to it.
Gary Gibson, 1998

50 Take Flight   ★ **F6c+**
12m The thin crack and arête to the right are harder than they look. A long reach may help.
Gary Gibson, Nick Taylor, 2002

The next three routes centre around the prominent arête up and to the right: this is actually above Cairn Sector, and they make great second pitches to The Misfits and Hissin' Sid. Gain them by scrambling carefully up the gully to below the left-hand side of the arête where there is a bolt belay. The routes get very little sunshine until late evening.

51 Buxton Goes French   **F6b+**
12m The slim face between the two wide cracks gives a very technical exercise if you can avoid touching the two cracks. F5+ if you don't!
Bill Birch, Jim Burton, 1994

52 Outer Limits   ★ **F6b**
12m A superb little pitch taking the left-hand side of the prominent arête. Photogenic at 9.30pm on a summer evening. Catch that glow!
Bill Birch, Nadim Siddiqui (both led), Jim Burton, 1994

53 The Twilight Zone   **F6a+**
11m The right-hand side of the arête proves surprisingly problematic.
Nadim Siddiqui, Bill Birch (both led), Jim Burton, 1994

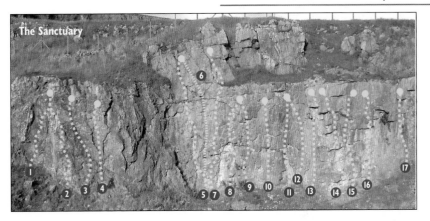

The Sanctuary

The Sanctuary

An interesting find tucked away around and to the right of Cairn Sector and above the Christian Salvessen depot. It offers a number of shorter and easier routes on excellent compact rock. It faces south-west, is relatively sheltered and receives sunshine from midday onwards although seepage will be a problem after long spells of rain.

The best approach to this cliff is by descending the slope below the end of Cairn Sector, behind the concrete posts alongside Breakfast at Safeways and walking left, facing out.

The first four routes lie on a crystalline wall at the left-hand side of the crag. These are nothing more than fillers-in.

① By Caesarean   **F5+**
10m The first wall taken direct. Some crunchy bits.
Gary Gibson, 2002

② New Arrivals   **F6a**
10m Just right again, starting up rib gains the same belay.
Gary Gibson, 2002

③ Expecting   **F4+**
10m Marginally better. A vague leftwards groove line.
Gary Gibson, 2002

④ Induction Program   **F5**
10m A steeper line, though no less juggy, to the right.
Gary Gibson, 2002

⑤ Safe Haven   **F5+**
18m This is the first of a trio of longer routes just right of a grassy flake / corner. Some hollow holds exist, so be careful.
Gary Gibson, 2001

⑥ The Hollow Man   **F5+**
18m A better and more direct line to the right to finish via an easier slab.
Gary Gibson, 2001

⑦ The Christian Salvage Man   ★ **F6a**
18m Named after the local security guard that you may meet. The better of the longer routes here. A small pillar and bulge lead to jug pulling up the wall and a crack to finish.
Gary & Hazel Gibson, 2001

⑧ Which Depp-Artment   **F6a+**
11m A short route taking an awkward bulge. Finish rightwards.
Gary Gibson, 2001

⑨ Ichabod   **F5**
11m An easier line on the wall to the right with a problematic finish.
Gary Gibson, 2001

⑩ Sleepy Hollow ★ F6a
11m A fine steep little pitch taking the vague blunt arête in the centre of the grey face on exquisite holds.
Gary & Hazel Gibson, 2001

⑪ Gone for a Tim Burton F5
11m A direct line up the jug-filled wall.
Gary Gibson, 2001

⑫ The Height Below F4+
11m Even easier up a brown streak just left of a wide crack.
Gary Gibson, 2002

⑬ The Sanctuarian F6c
11m This gains the left-hand side of the prominent overlap, with an evil crux through it.
Gary Gibson, 2001

⑭ For Haven's Sake ★ F6b
11m The first of a fine trio of routes to the right.
Gary Gibson, 2001

⑮ Downtown ★ F6b
11m Climb a wall to finish in a shallow groove. Pleasant.
Gary Gibson, 2001

⑯ What Lies Beneath ★ F6b
11m The final wall with an excellent finish.
Gary Gibson, 2001

⑰ Haven or Hell F6a+
9m An isolated pillar on the right with surprisingly steep moves. Short but worthwhile.
Gary Gibson, Jim Burton, 2002

The Dark Side

These walls are the continuation to the upper tier to the left of Papacy Buttress. From below Papacy Buttress keep walking past a subsidiary buttress until you turn the corner. The walls beyond are the Dark Side.

By name this section of cliff provides something of a paradox since these walls gain early morning sun-

shine to 12 noon and receive relatively little wind. Their recent development completes a series of cliffs at Harpur Hill Quarry that allow you to climb in the sunshine or shade throughout the day - a useful phenomenon around these parts. They do however develop some seepage after long periods of rain.

Towards the left-hand side of the face, as the cliff diminishes in height, is a small bay followed by the final grey wall just beyond.

① Endsville F6a
11m The first flat wall has a fingery finale.
Gary Gibson, Nick Taylor, 2002

② People Will Talk ★ F5
11m The pleasant arête in the left-hand side of the bay gives enjoyable climbing at the grade.
Gary Gibson, Nick Taylor, 2002

③ Parting of the Lips F5
11m The thin crack above the ledge on the left-hand side of the face at the back of the bay.
Gary Gibson, 2002

④ Ear to Ear F6a
12m The slim face to the left of the twin traditional cracks (both VS). One hard move / long reach.
Gary Gibson, Pete Clark , 2002

⑤ The Mouth Waters ★ F6c
12m The centre of the face. Excellent balance climbing.
Gary Gibson, Pete Clark, 2002

⑥ George Stark Calling ★ F6a+
12m The sharp arête tucked into the right-hand side of the bay. Climb it on its right-hand side.
Gary Gibson, Pete Clark, 2002

To the right is a prominent protruding face which contains the next couple of routes.

⑦ Stark Disbelief F6c+
15m Easy cracks lead to a blank-looking face. The holds may be subject to change whilst you are climbing this route! Excellent moves.
Gary Gibson, Pete Clark, 2002

8 **The Dark Half** ★ **F6b**

15m The prominent right-hand arête saves its difficulties for the moves off the half-height ledge.
Gary Gibson, 2002

9 **Graveyard Blues** **F6b**

11m An isolated arête to the right gives balance moves at half height.
Gary Gibson, 2002

10 **In Stark Contrast** ★ **F6c**

11m The high-level black wall. Technical excellence to the break. Steeper though easier above.
Gary & Hazel Gibson, 2002

A wall at a higher level gives three routes.

11 **Over the Deadline** ★ **F6b**

11m The left-hand line on the wall provides its best route. Fingery moves at half-height.
Gary Gibson, 2002

12 **Automatic Writing** **F6a+**

11m The centre of the wall passing a grassy ledge.
Gary Gibson, 2002

13 **Fool's Stuffing** **F6b**

11m The right-hand side of the inset wall. Avoiding the chimney may prove difficult.
Gary Gibson, 2002

Dominic Oughton on Unilateral Thinking, F6c
(page 134). Photo: Niall Grimes.

⑭ Pillar of Wisdom ★ F6b

11m The left-hand of three pillars gives a better route than its name might suggest. Start atop the grassy ledge system.
Gary Gibson, 2002

⑮ Invasion of the Creepazoid F6c+

18m A scary pitch via the central pillar. Fingery and reachy. Start atop the insecure blocks.
Gary Gibson, 2002

⑯ Later that Night F6a+

18m The right-hand of the three pillars with hard moves past the first two bolts. Use the crack on the left for a short section at mid-height.
Gary Gibson, 2002

⑰ The Coming of the Sparrows F5+

15m The slab right of the prominent corner is hardest at the start. Keep to the line of bolts.
Gary & Hazel Gibson, 2002

⑱ Stop the Pigeon F6b+

11m A little gem. Technical climbing up the black slab ends atop an obvious pillar. The line to the right of this is a pleasant HVS 5b, **Ken Dodd's Dad's Dog's Dead** (Nick Taylor).
Gary Gibson, Nick Taylor, 2002

⑲ Gathering Darkness F6c+

11m Climb direct up the smooth-looking slab to the right. A long reach may be essential.
Gary Gibson, 2002

⑳ A Trip on the Dark Side ★ F6a+

18m A long route up the centre of the wall. Good moves throughout with the difficulties around the 2nd bolt.
Gary & Hazel Gibson, 2002

㉑ Feel my Presence ★ F6b

16m Start via the corner before swinging right and up the satisfying arête. Better than it looks.
Gary Gibson, Jim Burton, 2002

Around to the right of the protruding buttress is an alcove and four pleasant routes.

㉒ Wild Olives ★ F6b+

18m Good wall climbing above the alcove to the left. A long reach helps through the main overlap. Try to stay on the arête at the top.
Gary Gibson, Nick Taylor, 2002

㉓ Gorignak ★ F6b

18m By starting through the prominent overhang to the right, the walls above give further good climbing. The crux lies at the top.
Gary Gibson, Nick Taylor, 2002

㉔ Omega 13 ★ F6a+

18m A long sustained wall climb to the right finishing via an obvious arête.
Gary & Hazel Gibson, 2002

㉕ Dr Lazarus F6a+

11m A short wide crack to the right leads to a difficult rightwards exit.
Gary Gibson, Nick Taylor, 2002

Route Index

Index

Index